THE STORY OF
MESA VERDE
NATIONAL PARK

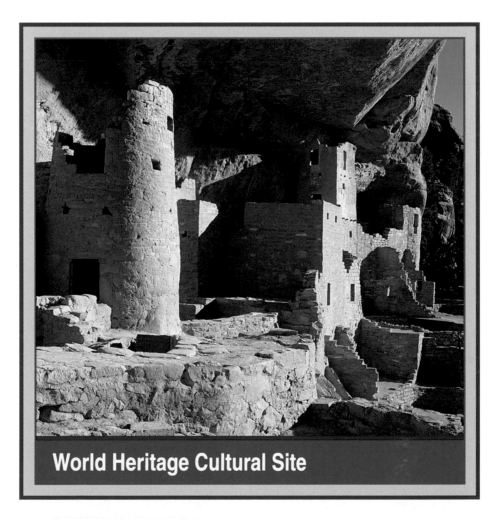

World Heritage Cultural Site

CHIEF PARK ARCHEOLOGIST, Retired
GILBERT R. WENGER
AUTHOR & PHOTOGRAPHER

DAVID W. WILSON
ILLUSTRATOR
MESA VERDE MUSEUM ASSOCIATION, INC.
PUBLISHER

First published in 1980 by Mesa Verde Museum Association, Inc.
Revised 1990/91 by the publisher.
Post Office Box 38, Mesa Verde National Park, Colorado 81330

ISBN 0–937062–15–4
Library of Congress card catalog number 90-61951

Manufactured in the United States of America.

First printing, 1980.
Reprinted: 1982, 1984, 1988, and 1990.
Revised and Reprinted, 1991.
Second revised printing, 1993.
Third revised printing, 1997.
Fourth revised printing, 1999.
Fifth revised printing, 2000.

11588   9/01

 Printed on Recycled Paper

TABLE OF CONTENTS

ABOUT THE AUTHOR

Photo: Marona

GILBERT R. WENGER'S career spanned 32 years with the National Park Service with his last 14 years being spent at Mesa Verde National Park as Chief Park Archeologist. He also served in archeological capacities at Tonto and Montezuma Castle National Monuments in Arizona. In 1972, Wenger was a member of the National Park Service Alaska Task Force to locate archeological areas that have since been included in the National Park System in Alaska.

Wenger, a native of Grand Junction, Colorado, received his Bachelor's and Master's Degrees at the University of Denver following his return from the Air Force in World War II. In other National Park Service assignments he worked at White Sands National Monument, New Mexico, Lake Mead National Recreation Area, Arizona-Nevada, and Mount Rushmore National Memorial, South Dakota. As a staff writer for the National Park Service Western Museum Laboratory in San Francisco, he wrote the exhibit content for twelve National Park Service Museums in the western United States.

Since his retirement he has actively continued giving lectures in archeology and Indian heritage to civic groups, schools, and universities both in the United States and Canada. He has tried to instill an appreciation for American Indian heritage and the critical need to help preserve archeological remains. He has authored numerous articles.

ACKNOWLEDGEMENTS

I WOULD LIKE to express my appreciation to the National Park Service and Mesa Verde National Park for permission to photograph Mesa Verde ruins and specimens and to use certain photographs in the preparation of this publication. I am indebted to Joyce Attebery, Dr. Robert Blair, and Stephen Wenger for their editorial suggestions.

I appreciate the support of the Mesa Verde Museum Association, Inc., Board of Directors: Clay Bader, Tom Hayden, Eugene Johnson, Tom Johnson, Dr. Edward Merritt, and Association Executive Director Rovilla Ellis.

MONTEZUMA VALLEY

160

Park Entrance

Point
Lookout

Montezuma Valley
Overlook

Morefield Village

MANCOS VA

Kilometers

Miles

Park
Point

MANCOS CANYON

Far View
Visitor Center

Mummy Lake
Far View
Ruins

MOREFIELD CANYON

PRATER CANYON

MOCCASIN MESA

Step House
Mug House

WETHERILL MESA

SPRUCE CANYON

CHAPIN MESA

Long House

Museum

Spruce Tree
House

Petroglyph
Point

Sun
Temple

Cliff Palace

Square Tower
House

Balcony House

UTE MOUNTAIN UTE
INDIAN RESERVATION

...help preserve these irreplaceable sites of antiquity if they are to be preserved for future generations.

INTRODUCTION

VISITORS TO MESA VERDE National Park are generally amazed by the number of cliff dwellings as well as the many fine artifacts they see. lt was similar interest by concerned individuals during the 1890s that ultimately led Congress to establish the area as a national park. Mesa Verde National Park is the largest archeological preserve in the United States and contains the greatest number of cliff dwellings ever found. Nearly 3,900 sites have been located within the park, and over 600 of these are cliff dwellings.

Mesa Verde was the center of the northern San Juan Anasazi (Pueblo) culture that existed in the Four Corners area for over a thousand years. There has been nearly a century of archeological investigation at Mesa Verde, varying from simple records kept by the Wetherill family who collected artifacts to very detailed excavations and technical reports by scientists from universities and institutions. The National Park Service personnel have done archeology in the park for a number of decades.

From the technical excavations and studies, it has been possible to reconstruct the life of the ancient Pueblo farmers who lived here for over seven centuries in what many would consider a harsh environment. These people became so skillful in finding ways to survive that they managed to expand from a simple hunting-gathering culture to a very complex society with thousands of people. Their succcess was attributable in part to the favorable topography and climate and to the flora and fauna. Equally important was their ability to grow corn, beans, and squash and to adapt to the local environment.

In September of 1978 the World Heritage Convention of the United Nations Educational, Scientific, and Cultural Organization selected Mesa Verde National Park to be a WORLD HERITAGE CULTURAL SITE in recognition of the significance of the ancient Pueblo culture that flourished here between the sixth and thirteenth centuries. This is indeed a unique honor of international importance, in that Mesa Verde was one of the first seven sites selected in the world for cultural recognition.

The scientific importance of Mesa Verde National Park makes it necessary for all who come here to help preserve these irreplaceable sites of antiquity for future generations.

The goal of this nontechnical publication is to help visitors better understand, enjoy, and appreciate the natural and human history of Mesa Verde National Park.

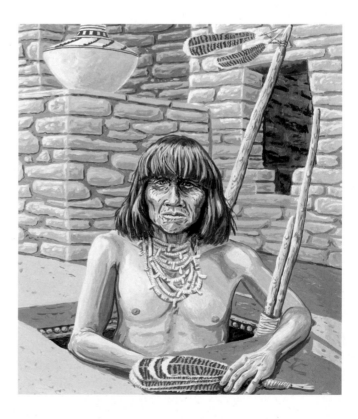

7

MAJOR DIVISIONS OF GEOLOGIC TIME

ERA		PERIOD
CENOZOIC *(Age of Recent Life)*	2.5(?)	Quaternary
		Tertiary
	63	
Mesa Verde geologic formation period		Cretaceous
MESOZOIC *(Age of Medieval Life)*		Jurassic
		Triassic
	230	
		Permian
		Pennsylvanian
		Mississipian
PALEOZOIC *(Age of Ancient Life)*		Devonian
		Silurian
		Ordovician
		Cambrian
	570	
PRECAMBRIAN		

Millions of Years before Present

*The geological
evolution of the
landscape created an
environment
favorable for man.*

MESA VERDE GEOLOGY

Cretaceous Seas 65 million years ago.

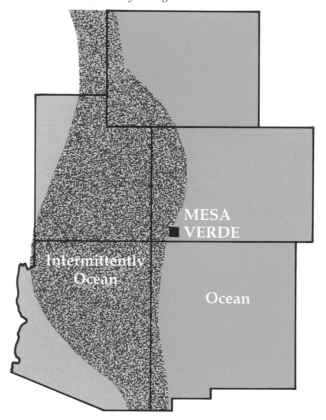

MESA VERDE

Intermittently Ocean

Ocean

T HE CREATION of this unique
environment took millions of years.
Ultimately it became rich in natural
resources that provided a favorable place for
humans to make their home. To appreciate the
changes this land has undergone, it is necessary to
go back 65 million years to Cretaceous times of the
Mesozoic Era. During late Cretaceous times a very
extensive sea covered the Great Plains and much
of what is now the Rocky Mountains. As can be
seen on the map depicting Cretaceous times, the
Four Corners area was in a zone that was
periodically covered by water as the seas
fluctuated in size over millions of years. The
oscillating nature of the shoreline changed the
local environment and the types of material
deposited.

*Above: Ripple marks left on ancient
seashore can be seen in Long House Ruin.*

*Left: Erosion has left the Mesa Verde upland
standing high above the valley floor.*

The oldest visible rock formation in the Park
is Mancos shale. Thousands of feet thick, it is
composed of consolidated mud and impure
limestone deposited in a quiet, relatively shallow
sea. Mancos shale is the gray bedrock seen along
the Park's entrance road where it climbs the big
hill to Morefield Campground.

The next geological event left between 80 and
125 feet (24 m to 38 m) of cross-bedded, marine-
deposited sand above the shale. Geologists believe
that much of this beach sand washed into the area
from streams that drained from the southwest as
the sea was withdrawing to the northeast. Known
as the Point Lookout sandstone, it is the huge
jutting mass of rock seen as visitors enter the Park.

These rocks later eroded into niches and alcoves where cliff dwellings would one day be constructed.

Various-sized alcoves formed by water erosion were frequently selected for sites in which to build houses protected from direct weather. Balcony House was built in one quite easy to defend if that need existed.

For another long period of time the shoreline continued to migrate toward the northeast. There was a large flood plain and in some places a swamp-like environment that existed in the Mesa Verde region. During this time over 300 feet (91 m) of lenticular sandstone beds with interbeds of siltstone and carbonaceous lenses were deposited. This sedimentary layer of rocks and resultant coal beds is called the Menefee formation; it is seen most easily just north of Balcony House on the canyon walls where layers of coal are exposed.

Again the sea advanced until the local region was on or near a shoreline. Great amounts of very fine-grained sand were laid down as beach sands or sand dunes. Horizontal bedding planes 20 to 30 feet (6 m to 9 m) apart were common. These rocks later eroded into niches and alcoves where cliff dwellings would one day be constructed. As might be expected, this formation is called the Cliff House sandstone, and it varies in thickness from 100 to 300 feet (30 m to 91 m). Because the sea and its shoreline were changing, there was considerable overlapping and interbedding of materials in the often repeated cycle of deposition.

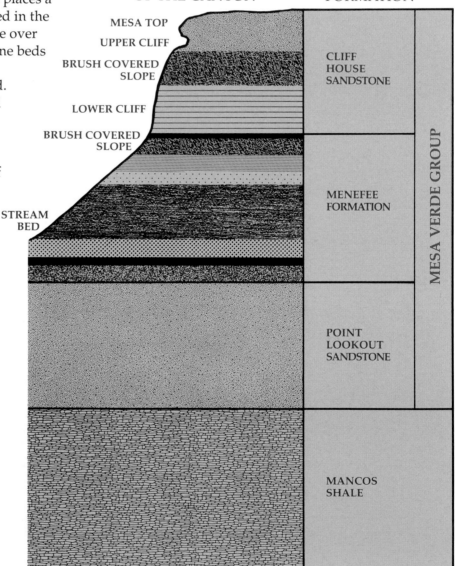

CROSS-SECTION OF THE CANYON
FORMATION

MESA TOP
UPPER CLIFF
BRUSH COVERED SLOPE

LOWER CLIFF
BRUSH COVERED SLOPE

STREAM BED

CLIFF HOUSE SANDSTONE

MENEFEE FORMATION

POINT LOOKOUT SANDSTONE

MANCOS SHALE

MESA VERDE GROUP

Ute Mountain south of Cortez resembles a reclining person wearing a feathered headdress. This mountain, formed from a volcanic uplift called a laccolith, is on the Ute Mountain Ute Indian Reservation.

Mesa Verde geology was greatly influenced during the Tertiary Period of the Cenozoic Era when the La Plata, West Elk, and Sleeping Ute Mountains were uplifted as laccolithic (mushroom-shaped) intrusive dome mountains. The San Juan Mountains were uplifted in the millions of years that followed and were eroded to a flat surface about 32 million years ago. The final uplift of the San Juan Mountains raised them thousands of feet above sea level; they have subsequently been dissected by glaciers and mountain streams.

The Mesa Verde was part of this uplift and was tilted in a somewhat bowl-shaped slope to the south. The erosion from the San Juan and La Plata Mountains deposited water-worn pebbles over parts of the Mesa Verde area. These pebbles are visible on the lower mesas of the plateau. Both Prater Canyon (heading at Montezuma Overlook) and Morefield Canyon (the campground valley) were formed at this time.

The rejuvenation of several streams running south-southwest cut through the sandstone layers of Tertiary deposits and into the Cretaceous shales. Erosion was so rapid that the headwaters of the streams in Prater and Morefield Canyons were cut off (beheaded) and subsequently dried up.

The head of Prater Canyon shows where the original stream was beheaded at the escarpment. Continued erosion has left the escarpment nearly 2,000 feet (610 m) above the valley floor.

Morefield Campground is located on the wide Morefield Canyon, formed by an earlier stream course that no longer exists.

Coupling their skills with the positive elements of the area, they began to live here about 1,500 years ago.

The highest elevation in Mesa Verde is Park Point at 8,572 feet (2613 m). From there one can easily see how the present plateau slopes gently to the south, where the elevation is about 6,000 feet (1829 m). The sharp edges of deeply-cut canyons formed by headward erosion during the past two million years stand out against the green forest. These streams, now only flowing intermittently, have left narrow strips of uplands or mesas between the canyons. Wind-blown deposits of reddish soils (loess) have covered the mesa tops, making them a fertile place for plants.

The geological evolution of the landscape created an environment favorable for humans. Coupling their own skills with the positive elements of the area, they began to live here about 1,500 years ago. It was the beginning of a 700 year period of habitation.

Inset: Wind-blown deposits of soil made the mesa tops a fertile place for agriculture.

Dozens of canyons dissect the Mesa Verde upland.

The study of tree rings and plant pollen reveals that the climate and vegetation have changed little from 600 years ago.

A Favorable Climate

MESA VERDE is classified as having a semi-arid (Steppe) climate. Such climates are generally dry and usually have a very limited natural water supply. Climatologist Trewartha says that Steppe climates are better suited for human habitation, but the unreliable rainfall makes the possibility of economic disaster a greater potential.

There are no rivers or running streams at Mesa Verde, and water runs in most canyons only following heavy summer thunderstorms or intermittently during spring snow melt. Despite the shortage of water, there were positive elements that made Mesa Verde a good place to live:

◢ A long, frost-free growing season (161-171 days).

◢ Moderately hot summer temperatures for crop growth.

◢ Reasonably dependable summer rains from mid-July through August.

◢ Moderately high daily temperatures in winter.

◢ Few severe cold periods in winter.

◢ Winter precipitation important for vegetation and ground water usually adequate.

◢ Soils suitable for growing crops in middle mesa areas.

◢ Springs.

Left: The large overhanging ledge protected Cliff Palace from winter snows.

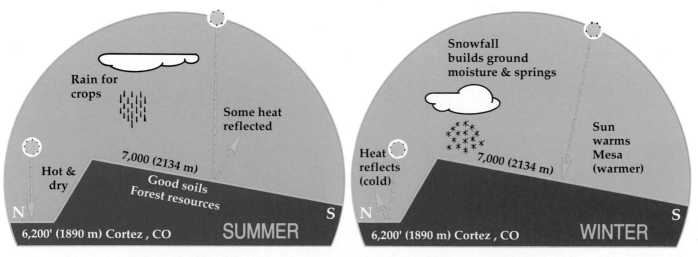

These two profiles show the major elements that made Mesa Verde an attractive place for humans to live in prehistoric times. High sun position in summer and low sun in winter.

Very observant of the storm patterns over the mesas, they chose the most suitable place to live — in the middle mesa areas around 7,000 feet elevation (2134 m).

Annual precipitation at Mesa Verde varies from 14 to 18 inches (36 cm to 46 cm), with most of it coming as snow between January and March. During average winters, 80 to 100 inches (203 cm to 254 cm) of snow may fall. But it is not uncommon for winters to bring little snow and to be quite dry. Knowing this, archaeologists have been interested in learning if the climate may have been different in prehistoric times. The study of tree rings and plant pollen reveals that climate and vegetation have changed little from 600 years ago. There have been several severe droughts since A.D. 1276, the last in the late 17th century.

The prehistoric Pueblo people, long experienced in growing crops, knew they had to have adequate rainfall if their corn, beans, and squash were to grow in sufficient quantity for an ever-increasing population. Very observant of the storm patterns over the mesas, they chose the most suitable place to live — in the middle mesa areas around 7,000 feet elevation (2134 m). Here there was usually sufficient rainfall, good temperatures for crop growth, and good, deep soil necessary for an agricultural livelihood. Numerous small springs and seeps provided drinking water.

Summer

Cool Breezes

During summer when the sun is nearly overhead, the sun's rays strike only the front walls, while back rooms remain very comfortable.

Cold Winds →

Winter

In winter when the low sun in the sky warms the stone masonry walls, heat is passed to other rooms and even to the cliff walls themselves. Supplemented by small fires in the rooms, less fuel is required than in a single dwelling not in a southwest facing cave.

Just as we try to plan for the best use of energy today, the topography of Mesa Verde made it a good place to live in prehistoric times because of its energy-related values. The higher north end of the mesas frequently receives more summer rainfall and winter snows than valleys below the escarpment, thus insuring a reasonable water supply. During the summer when the sun is directly overhead, the temperature is adequate for crops, but about 10 degrees cooler than in the hot valleys below the mesas. In the winter, when the sun is low in the southern sky, it shines further back into the south-southwest facing cliff dwellings to make them warm on non-cloudy afternoons. Winter temperatures are often 10 to 20 degrees warmer than in the Montezuma Valley below the northern escarpment, even though the valley is 600 feet (183 m) lower in elevation. The Pueblos were making good use of solar energy before Columbus arrived in the New World.

The name "Mesa Verde" was given by 16th century Spanish explorers. It means "green table".

THE GREEN OF MESA VERDE

THE TOPOGRAPHY of Mesa Verde offers the visitor a chance to easily see several different types of plant communities. Three important controls that govern where certain species of plants will grow are temperature, moisture, and soil. Elevation affects temperature and moisture; thus, changes in elevation are reflected by changes in plant communities.

At higher elevations in the Park where winter snowfall is heaviest and moisture more abundant, we find the biggest trees. Douglas fir stand high above the mountain brush along the upper canyons and the steep northern escarpment. Some Douglas fir are also found in canyon bottoms where there is adequate moisture. Ponderosa pine dot Morefield Canyon, and in isolated places above 8,000 feet (2438 m) some quaking aspen grow.

Across the entire width of the Park, parallel to the north rim and extending several miles downslope to the south, is the mountain-brush community composed of Gambel oak serviceberry, and mountain mahogany. On the east side of the Park is a scattering of piñon-juniper in the patchwork of oak. Nearly pure oak and serviceberry mark the western side of the Park. The mountain brush zone is a favorite habitat for Rocky Mountain mule deer, but in winter it is usually covered with deep snow. It is unlikely that prehistoric people made any attempt to live here, even though the oak did provide food and resources for them.

In spring, serviceberry and fendler bush add a white and cream brilliance to the background color of oak. The ground comes alive with bright yellow, red, lavender, and blue, as flowering plants burst into bloom. In the fall the first frost turns the oak to yellow, orange, and red, as if nature were celebrating the change of season. Soils of the mountain brush zone are generally shallow and heavily mixed with broken rock fragments that help hold the moisture.

Upper left: Gambel oak in full fall brilliance.
Lower left: Yarrow and Scarlet Gilia.

Above: Prickly Pear cactus.
Right: Fendler bush.

Utah juniper, so common in the Park, was widely used. Being a hard wood, it made excellent tools. The blue-green berries were edible if mixed with other foods. The berries were also used for medicinal purposes.

The piñon pine provided wood for house construction, tools, and firewood. Its nuts were a good source of protein.

Right: Typical canyon topography at Mesa Verde.

Inset: Lightning-caused fire on Moccasin Mesa. It is quite likely that prehistoric farmers cleared so many acres of forest for farm lands that such intense fires as this did not occur when they lived on Mesa Verde.

Juniper berries were used as food supplements, as flavoring, and in medicine.

The dominant vegetation in Mesa Verde is the piñon-juniper forest. It extends from about 7,800 feet (2377 m) elevation in the north all the way to the southern boundary of the Park, and covers nearly all mesas and many of the slopes of the upper canyons. Although the piñon pine or Utah juniper seldom exceed 30 feet (9 m) in height, they were used in house construction by the ancient Anasazi. Both trees also provided firewood and good wood for a variety of tools. If there is adequate moisture, piñon pine will produce a crop of nuts every several years, a very edible food used by the Indians. Juniper berries were used as food supplements, as flavoring, and in medicine. The soil of this forest zone is a moderately deep, rich loam, containing red loess, a wind-blown soil excellent for agriculture.

The piñon-juniper forest is comparatively dense, but much downed timber and mutton grass make it especially vulnerable to lightning-caused fires. When devastating fires occur, 200 to 300 years will pass before the piñon-juniper forest again matures.

The last major plant community is that of the canyons. One immediately notices the lack of trees and the dominance of gray-green vegetation that mark the heavy growth of big sagebrush, the climax plant of the canyon bottoms. Cheatgrass, flowering plants, and cactus grow in between. There is usually a distinct boundary between the big sagebrush and the piñon-juniper found on canyon slopes. Soils of the canyon bottom are sandy loam, a deep, coarse-textured soil resulting from wind and water sorted sediments. Soil moisture is very low, which drastically restricts plants not having deep roots such as big sagebrush. Big sagebrush is rich in an aroma that is long remembered. It also grows in the open glades on the mesas where old fires have burned off the forest and does well in the transition zone between the mountain brush and the piñon-juniper in locations such as Far View Ruins.

These three plant communities, the mountain brush, piñon-juniper, and big sagebrush, possess distinct characteristics of the different plant zones, and each offers important relationships in the total ecosystem of the area.

Animals were a resource for food, and the bones were used for tools by men and women in their daily activities.

THE WILDLIFE OF MESA VERDE

MESA VERDE, a relatively isolated upland, has a moderately diversified animal population. Animals live in preferred habitats that are closely related to vegetation types. Some are affected by other types of animals living in the same region. Populations are established by the specific animal and its particular food needs. To the prehistoric Pueblo people, the animals constituted a valuable resource from which they could fashion tools, clothing, and food.

The Rocky Mountain mule deer is the common and abundant large animal at Mesa Verde National Park. When driving the park roads, visitors will most often see the deer in the early morning or evening hours. A favorite habitat for mule deer is the oak community where there is excellent browse and, in the fall, acorns. Campers at Morefield see deer browsing, apparently unconcerned by humans. In the late fall, bucks with large antlers are often seen around the Far View area. When winter snows start to fall, most deer seek trails leading to the lower and deeper canyons or go over the north rim of the escarpment into the piñon-juniper forest below.

Above: Rocky Mountain mule deer.

Below: Animal designs from Classic Mesa Verde pottery.

Long before Columbus discovered America, the Pueblo people were raising turkeys for feathers from which they made feather-wrapped yucca cordage blankets.

Right: Wild Merriam turkey.

Below: Steller's jay.

In recent years a number of elk have been seen in the upper canyons along the escarpment. About three dozen have lived in the Park for over a decade. Both black bear and mountain lion (cougar) have become more common in the past few years. Coyotes live all over the park and are seen along some roads. Usually coyotes are heard about sunrise. Bobcats, badgers, and the gray fox live here, but are rarely seen except by Park employee residents. A few bighorn sheep live in the isolated canyons, but a visitor is lucky to see one.

By far the most common small animals are the gray rock squirrel and chipmunks. Some tassel-eared squirrels live in Spruce Canyon and along the escarpment. In some years cottontail rabbits are very numerous.

Because the Park is in a transition zone between the lower deserts and the high mountains of the southern Rockies, many birds either live here or migrate through the Park every year. Long before Columbus discovered America, the Pueblo people were raising turkeys for feathers from which they made feather-wrapped yucca cordage blankets. This was a practice that continued for hundreds of years. By the turn of the present century, only a few turkeys remained and during the early days of Park exploration, many surviving turkeys were shot by hunters. Some years later the National Park Service reintroduced the native turkey.

Above: Turkey vultures with a six foot (2 m) wing span are often seen April to October, soaring over the mesas and canyons searching for carrion.

Left: Relatively common at Mesa Verde, Bailey's collared lizard eats insects, other small lizards, and plant foods.

Between April and October, turkey vultures can be seen daily, riding the air currents above the canyons. From observations, it appears these large birds with a wing span of over five feet (2 m) are decreasing too. In early spring the Park staff welcomes the return of the vultures, as it means winter is over. These large birds serve to keep the area free from decaying animals that die from various causes.

Very large flocks of ravens are seen in the summer, but only a few stay all winter. Some of the other large birds which reside in the Park are red-tailed hawks, sharp-shinned hawks, a few golden eagles, and western horned owls. With the exception of the owls, most of these are seen along the northern escarpment.

It is very common when walking through the trees to hear the noisiest bird in the piñon-juniper forest screaming his call. It is the Steller's jay. It can be distinguished by its dark blue color and the crest on its head. In winter piñon and scrub jays often live in the Park in large numbers, but most leave in summer.

Chickadees, titmice, and nuthatches frequent the Park, as do towhees and warblers. In summer, black-chinned, broad-tailed, and rufous hummingbirds dart from flower to flower seeking nectar.

Along almost every trail to a cliff dwelling, youngsters in particular will notice lizards scurrying from rock to rock. Some will see the pretty collared lizard, though there are many other smaller kinds too. Rattlesnakes are seldom seen along popularly used trails, but they do live in the area. They are most often seen along the escarpment. In the fall, when it starts to turn cold, tarantulas frequently cross the highways or the forest floor seeking a hole they can crawl into to hibernate for the winter. They are not poisonous, but handling them is not suggested.

The large nonpoisonous hairy tarantula (2 inch [5 cm] leg-span) feeds on a variety of insects. It is most often seen in the fall.

"Anasazi", a Navajo word meaning "Ancient Ones", is used by archeologists to identify prehistoric Pueblo people.

EARLY HUMANS & THE BASKETMAKERS

J UST as it is necessary to describe the geographical area surrounding Mesa Verde to understand the geology, it is important to recognize that the cultural development of the ancient people at Mesa Verde is part of a much larger cultural relationship. The growth of the Anasazi (Pueblo) culture involved centuries of development and change over a large portion of the Four Corners area. When one looks at Mesa Verde's large cliff dwellings and the earlier sites, it is only natural to wonder where these people came from and who their ancestors were.

It is known that as early as 10,000 years ago early hunters roamed over a great expanse of land on the Colorado Plateau. The terrain restricted the movement of people. It is a vast region of deep canyons, isolated land forms, limited water, sparse vegetation, and few animals. Such barriers naturally limited the size and number of hunting groups, but archeologists have found small campsites and distinctive spear points where these hunters have been. The presence of Folsom hunters has been confirmed at Folsom in northeastern New Mexico, although evidence of these hunters has not been found within 50 miles (80 km) of Mesa Verde. This phase of early hunters is graphically shown in the first diorama in the Park museum.

Left: Extensive trading between Indians of local and more distant villages introduced new items, and perhaps new foods and new ideas.

Early humans in the New World — the Folsom hunters.

These early hunters had to utilize anything they could find that was edible to supplement animal meat. Skilled in gathering seeds, fruits, and nuts from plants, these hunter-gatherers existed for several thousand years before a new plant was to change their way of life. About 2000 years ago, corn was introduced from Meso-America through trading, and these hunter-gatherers settled into a more sedentary way of life. It was the beginning of agriculture in southwestern Colorado. These people, called Basketmakers, were living in the area around, but *not in,* Mesa Verde by A.D. 1.

The Basketmakers were the ancestral base for the people who lived at Mesa Verde. It is vital to understand this early phase to better grasp later cultural changes. The word "Anasazi" is a Navajo word meaning "Ancient Ones". Archeologists use the term to identify the prehistoric Pueblo peoples of this area.

This replica of White Dog Cave in northeastern Arizona accurately shows how the Basketmakers lived in rock shelters. The stone-lined cists were for food storage.

The Basketmakers

A.D. 1 - A.D. 550

Archeologists working in the northeastern part of Arizona, northwestern New Mexico, southeastern Utah, and southwestern Colorado (the Four Corners area) around the turn of the century recognized artifacts which they identified as having been made by a simple hunting-gathering culture. The most outstanding skill of these people was shown in the excellent baskets they constructed. The name "Basketmaker" was applied to their culture.

These people favored large and small shallow rock shelters where a family or two could seek protection from the elements. Even though rock shelters are found in and around Mesa Verde, no Basketmaker sites of this early period have been found in the Park. It is unknown why they did not live here. Perhaps at that stage of their

development they simply could not handle the normally stormy winters. There is little likelihood that their habitations might be covered by the large cliff dwellings of later periods, as none have been found in empty rock shelters that would easily have served as a place for them to live. Dry caves in other areas gave much protection to items left by Basketmakers, so archeologists have a good understanding of their culture.

The Basketmakers were a little over five feet tall (1.5 m) with black hair. Mummies found in dry caves occupied by these people show the women cut their hair short and the men allowed their hair to grow long. Some men had elaborate hair styles and often tied their hair in three sections. One went down each side and one down the back. Items made with human

hair suggest that it was commonly used for weaving.

Some mummies have been found, but the bodies were not intentionally mummified. When the dead were buried in a very dry cave, the dry soil dehydrated the body. Bacteria that would otherwise decay it could not live in such dry soil.

Food was a constant, primary concern for the Basketmakers. Like the earlier hunting cultures of the Colorado Plateau, these people were masters at collecting seed, nuts, and other fruits and berries. With corn available to cultivate, the people began to stay longer in the area. They found that some species of gourds grew well in gardens, thus providing another food. We know they were competent hunters by the tools they fashioned from the bones of animals.

A man practices using the atlatl for hunting.

The atlatl, while somewhat crude, is actually a very inventive weapon. Basically, the shaft-holder for the spear increased the length of the throwing arm so the user could propel the spear, armed with a detachable dart, with great force. Practice was very important, as the atlatl was an inaccurate weapon compared to the bow and arrow that would be used in later times.

Baskets were most important to these people, as they served so many different uses. Constructed in a coiled technique, they were used to store foods and treasured items. Some baskets were coated with pitch on the inside to help seal them so they would hold water. Baskets thus provided another means to cook food other than roasting over coals. The Basketmakers would heat stones in the fire and then drop them into the pitch-coated baskets to heat water. Hot stones would have to be added several times to cook anything substantial. Charred, shallow, flat baskets have been found, and it appears they were used to roast or parch seeds by placing hot coals in with the seeds and then shaking them together. Proficiency would be required or the basket would probably be burned beyond use.

The Basketmakers made excellent baskets in many different shapes and sizes.

The Basketmakers made many small woven bags to carry and store things. These twined, woven bags were often pointed or round on the bottom. They were soft and often had designs painted on them rather than woven into the bag.

Twined woven bag.

*An important article
of Basketmaker clothing
was the sandal.*

*Far Right: This is the most fabulous
collection of woven belts ever found in the
Southwest. The Basketmakers obtained
hair from their dogs to make these belts.*

*Sandals were made from yucca fiber
and leaves.*

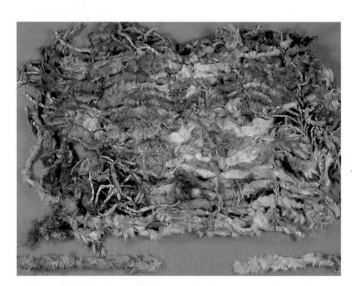

*Rabbit fur blanket
fragment.*

The Basketmakers liked
beads for body ornaments.
Many of those found were made
of shells, indicating the people
traded with others who had
contact with people near the
Pacific Ocean.

Most Basketmaker rock
shelter sites have the remains of
stone-lined storage cists. A
circular hole was dug several
feet into the ground and lined
around the inside edge with
vertically placed flat slabs of
rock to hold the dirt out. Small
logs were used to cover the cist,
with a flat stone placed over the
opening in the top to protect
food stored inside. Such storage
areas helped the Basketmakers
save enough food for the
winters. In some sites the bones
of humans have been found,
suggesting that when cists were
no longer used or a site was
abandoned, they served as a
burial place. Items such as
sandals, axes, digging sticks, and
ornaments are commonly found
in graves so it is possible the
people believed the deceased
might need them in the
"hereafter".

An important article of
Basketmaker clothing was the
sandal. The rocky terrain of the
canyon country was hard on feet.
Many hundreds of sandals or
fragments have been found in
Basketmaker sites that show all
degrees of wear.

Few fragments of
Basketmaker clothing have been
uncovered even in good
Basketmaker sites. Little is
known about what they wore.

Some yucca aprons have
been found and may have been
worn by women during their
menstrual periods. Men's
clothing probably consisted of a
G-string and sandals. During
cold weather, blankets fashioned
from yucca cordage and strips of
rabbit fur were very popular;
and many fragments of these
have been found in Basketmaker
sites.

A new house type and the introduction of pottery are two very significant differences to be noted for this later period.

THE MODIFIED BASKETMAKERS

A.D. 550 - A.D. 750

A FTER SEVERAL HUNDRED YEARS of slow advancement, the Basketmakers' increasing dependence upon agriculture forced them to gradually abandon their semi-nomadic way of life. Even though raising corn and squash enabled them to remain in one area, they obviously were always looking for a better place to live. It is very likely that Basketmaker people climbed the northern escarpment of Mesa Verde or came up one of the many canyons from the south while hunting food or game animals and found the area to be a suitable place to build their homes. They found a water supply of seeps and springs and good soil for growing crops. Above all, there was an abundant supply of wood for fires, house construction, and tools.

This movement occurred about A.D. 550 and is the first evidence of human use of Mesa Verde. Archeologists call the later phase the Modified Basketmakers. Two very significant differences are to be noted for this later period: a new house type and the introduction of pottery.

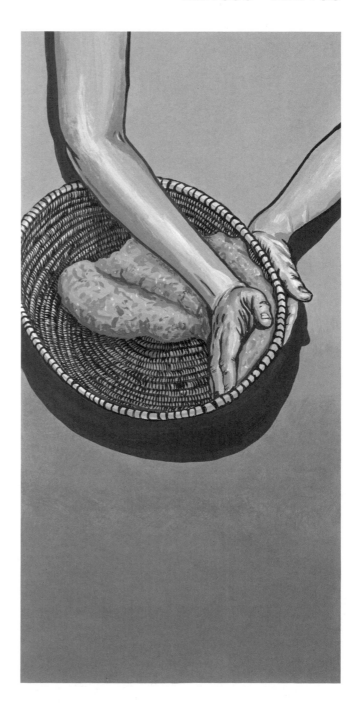

Left: Pithouses were built in Step House on Wetherill Mesa as here depicted in this diorama.

Right: The basketry imprint in the fire-hardened clay suggests the people were experimenting and trying to make a watertight container. Such trial and error experiments led to the development of usable pottery.

33

Cutaway view of pithouse model to show construction techniques.

Pithouses

The people began the construction of permanent, semi-subterranean pithouses. It is quite common to find clusters of pithouses on the mesa tops, showing that the people preferred to live in small villages rather than alone in single units. Almost all of these pithouses consisted of a large living room and a smaller antechamber. Using stone and wooden tools, the people dug a rounded or oblong-shaped depression several feet into the ground. Usually there was a low bench surrounding the floor area with four timbers placed in holes in each corner to support a roof framework. Timbers were placed across the tops of the four posts with smaller logs, sticks, juniper bark, and mud to cover the framework to make it weatherproof.

The larger room, used as sleeping quarters and a general work area, was divided into two sections by a low wall extending toward the firepit. Utensils and other implements for food preparation are often found behind this low wall, and the antechamber was probably a large storage area. Entrance to the pithouse was by means of a ladder through an opening in the roof above the centrally located firepit.

There are reasons to believe that the ceremonial rituals of the two later periods had their beginnings in the pithouse. In most pithouses there is a small hole in the floor between the firepit and the north wall. (Some Pueblo Indians believe this hole to be a symbolic opening to the underworld.) In the later ceremonial chambers, it is called the Sipapu (see-pah-pu).

Below: Floor plan of Modified Basketmaker pithouse.

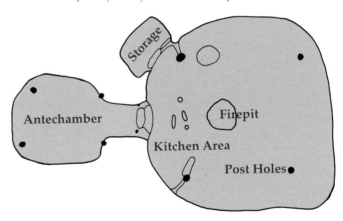

Another opening to the antechamber from the roof is believed to have been used for ventilation and to supply air to the fire. When there was no antechamber a vertical shaft to the outside surface allowed air to enter the house proper. A stone slab set in the small passageway between the antechamber or ventilator, if there was one, served as a deflector or baffle to help distribute the air around the fire.

When archeologists excavated these houses centuries later, they noted that most pithouses had burned. With so much wood used in house construction, it is easy to understand how quickly the wood dried from fires used for heating and cooking in the house. There were probably a number of house fires caused by carelessness. There is a possibility that if someone died in the house, custom may have required the house to be burned. It is not generally believed that fires were started by an enemy.

Beans in Agriculture

The bean, a new plant of great importance, made its appearance at this time. This protein-rich food was surely welcomed by the people. As in previous times, the digging stick remained a very familiar tool in the cultivation of crops on the mesas.

Women spent considerable effort in modifying natural plants, seeds, nuts, and berries to make them suitable for food.

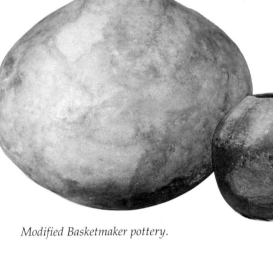

Modified Basketmaker pottery.

Pottery

Pottery was probably the most important new invention. It completely changed cooking and eating habits. Food could be cooked more thoroughly and was more palatable. It also allowed the use of many other forms of food, adding a greater variety to the diet.

The first pottery shapes were simple. It is most likely the people copied shapes from gourds that grew in their gardens. Much of the pottery was a plain gray color, and only near the end of Modified Basketmaker times were crude designs added. While pottery became more and more popular, baskets were still used, but fewer were produced. Some of the large multicolored carrying and storage baskets exceeded the quality of any produced after. Bags were no longer woven, as pottery functioned better for storage.

Above: 1300-year-old storage basket.

Below: Carrying baskets.

Woman's apron.

Hunting Weapons

The bow and arrow began to replace the atlatl as a hunting weapon. It was far more accurate and brought more success to the hunter. The curved throwing or hunting stick, similar to the type used by the Hopi, continued to be used.

Clothing

Clothing improved during Modified Basketmaker times, but still there was not a great deal worn. More animals could be obtained with the bow and arrow, so more animal skins were used. A sudden switch from rabbit fur blankets to turkey-feather blankets may have been caused by over-hunting of rabbits. Turkeys were easier to control in that they were nearly domesticated and the feathers more readily available. Women twined turkey feathers around yucca cordage to make robes and blankets for winter use. Men wore a breech cloth and women a small apron. The scalloped sandal replaced earlier types.

Sandals were vital to protect feet from rocky terrain, cactus, and insects.

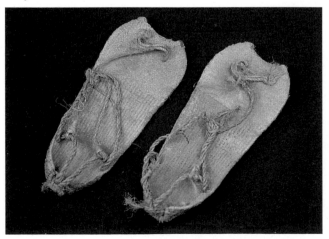

Besides furnishing food, many articles or tools could be fashioned from bighorn sheep.

The Use of Natural Resources

Nearly all material resources available were utilized to make living easier. Animal bones were shaped into bone awls for sewing and skin scrapers for removing meat from hides. Turkey bones, which are hollow, were often made into necklaces. Stone, bone, and shells obtained through trade were made into attractive jewelry for decorative purposes.

Because Mesa Verde lacks suitable stone for making projectile points and other stone tools, excursions had to be made to the Mancos River or the distant mountains to obtain harder rock than the sandstone of Mesa Verde. From the harder stone, knives, drills, scrapers, and other tools were chipped with the use of deer antler tips. Grooved stone axes and mauls were also made from granite and igneous rocks. The most common stone tools

in use every day of the year were metates and manos. These stones were used to grind meal and flour from corn, nuts, berries, and other food. Some of the food was formed into patties that could be dried and kept for winter.

Nearly every able person probably had to do some kind of work if the families were to have the things they needed to survive. Mothers fastened and carried their babies in an oblong, flexible cradle with a soft head pad made of juniper bark to protect the child's head.

Considerably advanced in technology from the early hunters, the Modified Basketmakers had a much better life than their ancestors. Their culture was to develop and progress more rapidly with better homes and the introduction of pottery.

Typical Basketmaker trough metate and mano.

A baby cradle.

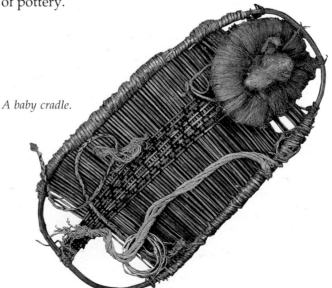

Improvements in architecture, pottery, and religious direction helped the Pueblo people gain a better way of life.

THE DEVELOPMENTAL PUEBLO

A.D. 750 - A.D. 1100

THE PERIOD starting about A.D. 750 saw the beginning of the Pueblo pattern of life that we are familiar with today. The Pueblo were direct descendants of the earlier Basketmakers. This culture evolved quite rapidly with new ideas, improved technology, and new architectural forms.

When archeologists began to study the many Anasazi (Pueblo) sites, they noticed many changes starting about A.D. 750. They found human burials with different shaped craniums (heads), and some archeologists speculated that perhaps a new people had moved into the Basketmaker territory and eliminated the earlier people. They soon realized that in actuality the people were the same. Through the use of the hard board cradle the cranium was flattened on the back as a result of the baby having its head securely tied to the cradle. The change from the earlier soft padded cradle probably occurred because more women had to work to support the families. The only way women with tiny babies could work was to take their babies with them; to protect the baby's fragile neck, the head was fastened to the rigid cradle. This continued pressure on the soft skull flattened the rear of it. As the skull hardened, the deformity became permanent.

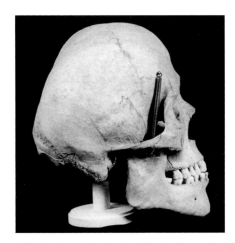

Flattening of the back of the skull resulted in a broad face, a look that became very stylish.

The most obvious change was in the architecture of their houses. The change clearly directs attention to a more formalized kinship, social, and religious pattern. In place of pithouses the people began to construct surface dwellings. These first houses had vertical walls, were flat-roofed, and were joined together in long rows. Nearly all houses faced to the south or southwest. Sometimes there were smaller rooms behind the main house that were used for storage.

In front of these villages the Pueblo farmers frequently dug one or more subterranean pitrooms, which served as club rooms and for special societies or ceremonial use. Four vertical posts held up the roof, and a ventilation shaft allowed air to enter the room. More and more of these deep pitrooms began to function for planned religious activities, including prayers for rain and sunshine for their crops. Since food was increasingly important to a larger population, a greater emphasis was placed upon specific rituals for gardening success.

Left: Villages like these built about A.D. 850 have been found on both Chapin and Wetherill Mesas.

This sequence clearly illustrates how the earlier Modified Basketmaker pithouse evolved in two directions; the above-ground structure developed into houses and the pit evolved into the kiva.

Before the period was over, the underground pitroom's oblong shape changed to a round chamber, the beginning of the traditional shape for Pueblo kivas. Within these kivas greater religious emphasis began to provide for the spiritual needs of the people. Special societies whose importance reached a peak in Classic Pueblo times have their roots here.

Stones began to be used more in construction of dwellings, and the houses were built with contiguous walls to suggest social changes that affected more people than a single family. These house units often took on the shape of an L, U, or E, sometimes around a plaza. By A.D. 1075 the Pueblo people added a second stone to the width of their walls, thus making them strong enough to support rooms more than one story high. Trash dumps, which accumulated at all villages, were generally south of the village and began to form sizeable mounds. Sometimes trash areas were used as burial places, a practice that will be explained later.

About this same time, the Pueblo people seemed to come under some sort of tension; they began to construct towers, either as part of the house or the village. Towers built near kivas and connected with underground tunnels were possibly used in relation to religion. Other towers gave the impression that they may have been

lookouts. Today most of the tower remains stand less than 10 feet (3 m) tall, with crumbled stones at their base. Few exceeded 15 feet (5 m) when they were used. Since the piñon-juniper forest stands higher than this, how could they be lookouts? It must be remembered that centuries of farming had taken place before the building of the towers, so much of the forest was probably already cleared, making the area somewhat open.

As the population increased, more villages were built. The problem of obtaining enough food for all became more critical, and it seems that there were community efforts rather than single family attempts to grow more crops. Where the single kiva served the extended family, the larger villages might require several kivas or a large one. For example, in Morefield Canyon a kiva 55 feet (17 m) in diameter has been found and partially excavated. Such large kivas would involve many people for construction alone, and its large size discloses a preplanned effort. Community support would be needed to complete such projects.

Artist's conception of how one village of this period may have looked when lived in by Pueblo people.

The Morefield kiva is the largest found at Mesa Verde. Since it is not accessible to visitors, it was backfilled with dirt to protect it for the future.

Typical Mesa Verde Kiva:

16'
(5 m)

Morefield Kiva 55 ft.
(17 m)

A check-gate system allowed the users to divert water either into the reservoir or down a by-pass ditch. Due to repeated short-term droughts, the reservoir may never have been as successful as planned.

The silt, which was often several feet deep, would retain moisture for a considerable period of time. The Pueblo farmers used those areas as small farming plots.

An aerial view of the reservoir at Far View.

Water Conservation

Several water management projects are other examples of group involvement. Near Far View House a large doughnut-shaped depression was found before 1900. Its purpose was soon recognized as a prehistoric reservoir. Located about 600 feet (183 m) northwest of Far View House, this water storage reservoir, 90 feet in diameter (27 m), could not have been built without community effort. It was nearly 12 feet deep (4 m), and the outside walls were made of stone with mud mortar. A ditch ran down the ridge from a higher elevation to fill the reservoir. Small ditches converged to feed the larger ditch. Unfortunately, the original ditch was not recognized; it was covered by the building of the road many decades ago.

The importance of having a dependable water supply near the village was realized long before the people started to move into the canyons to build cliff dwellings. Scooped out of the mesa top, the reservoir served primarily as a domestic water supply for nearby Far View House and others in the immediate area. What appears to be another reservoir is located on an adjoining mesa top one mile west. There is one additional reservoir of large size in Morefield Canyon, but it was not lined with stones as was the reservoir for Far View.

The Pueblo used another type of water control in the form of check dams. These were not water conservation devices, per se, but rather were silt-retaining dams. Intermittent water running down the small drainage courses deposited silt behind the dams. The silt, which was often several feet deep, would retain moisture for a considerable period of time. The Pueblo farmers used those areas as small farming plots.

The Pueblo people made extensive use of check dam farming plots for planting early corn since those areas were more likely to be frost-free than the large open areas.

Most pottery was made for specific purposes such as seed jars, water canteens, ladles, bowls, and jars.

Pottery

Making pottery must have been enjoyable during Developmental Pueblo times. With a more substantial food supply, the potter had freedom to experiment with new techniques. Many new shapes and new types of surface finish and decorations came into use.

Excavations of early Pueblo sites uncovered many miniature vessels. Perhaps they were a fad to the earlier people, much as sub-miniatures are today. Possibly the potter was trying new shapes, or perhaps young potters may have been taught pottery making by such miniatures. Many odd-shaped pieces were found, but most of them were not very practical for surviving any moderate use. Some of the vessels appear to be canteens or pitchers. The half-gourd-shaped ladles were eating or drinking vessels.

With a more substantial food supply, the potter had freedom to experiment with new techniques.

Both shallow and steep-sided bowls were made. Judging from the number found in ruins, the shallow ones were more popular. The first cooking jars closely resemble those made in Modified Basketmaker times. The pottery was made by shaping the base of the vessel in a basket or upon another bowl and building up the sides by adding a wide band of clay. Bowls were smoothed out to give the vessel a plain, smooth surface.

A popular technique was to smooth all of the vessel except the bands near the neck, which were left for decoration. The technique of using bands of clay may have led to using ropes of clay and leaving them pronounced instead of smoothing them flat. The coils were pinched rather than pressed smooth, giving the vessel a corrugated surface. These vessels were mainly used for cooking and food storage. Corrugated vessels were to continue in use for the next 300 years at Mesa Verde.

A second tradition becoming common was a white pottery with black design. Until A.D. 1050 the potter found a clay rich in iron and used it as a basis for black paint. From that time on they seemed to have preferred to use plant materials that made a good carbon pigment. This new decorative effort became prominent in Anasazi ceramics.

As time went on there was a great refinement of shapes and decorative paint. The odd-shaped vessels were no longer made, although some later vessels take on anthropomorphic forms. Some of these probably served special purposes. One large watermelon-shaped vessel had a small opening at one end and was probably used for seed storage. The potter painted it with attractive designs.

Bowls, pitchers, ladles, canteens, and water and seed jars were the common forms in use. Some very large decorated and undecorated vessels have been found. These were used for food storage. The Pueblo people knew they had to store food for the long, cold winters.

Wide-mouth pitchers used for drinking were modified as time went on. They evolved into the mugs so common throughout the rest of Anasazi times. The half-gourd-shaped ladles became larger, with strap and bar handles. These were very common around every cooking area. Strap handles were applied to large bowls, most of which had indented bases.

Note the use of designs on the pottery of this period. The canteen-shaped vessel below has a centipede painted on the handles. Geometric patterns were widely used. Some effigy-shaped vessels occurred, but not in great numbers. Small water jars with small loop handles were hung to keep them out of the way. Fired clay pipes with large flares have been found, but none contain true tobacco ash. Other uniquely shaped pieces were used to hold treasured trinkets. Decorated miniatures were also made.

Manos and metates (grinders), digging sticks, and most basic tools needed in everyday living continued to be made, but in larger quantities than before. The bow and arrow was the primary weapon for defense or hunting. Long, narrow stone projectile points were fastened on arrow shafts. Cotton was traded into the area and some was woven into small cotton blankets and breech cloths. Sandals were slightly improved. Turkey-feather blankets continued to be used. Ornaments made from various nonlocal materials show that extensive trading was occurring. While all of these improvements helped the Pueblo people live a better life, the changes in architecture, pottery, and religious direction were the most important.

The many different shapes of pottery suggests a period of great experimentation.

In the Golden Age of the Anasazi at Mesa Verde, great advancements were made in architecture and pottery.

THE CLASSIC OR GREAT PUEBLO PERIOD

A.D. 1100 - A.D. 1300

MOST VISITORS to Mesa Verde National Park are eager to see and visit the large cliff dwellings that represent the best of Mesa Verde's ancient Pueblo architecture. The building of large community houses required the cooperation of many people. The beautiful pottery and other craft items are impressive, achieving their greatest refinement during Classic Pueblo times. While this was a good time, it was to become a time of concern for the Pueblo people as farming became more crucial to provide food for a peak population of about 5,000 persons.

Numerous small unit pueblos were abandoned in favor of moderately large community houses or villages. Part of this was simply the result of the people learning how to build better homes. Archeologists feel the tension experienced during the Developmental Period was evidenced by better constructed houses that could easily be defended and protected if necessary. The masonry became excellent as the builders shaped the sandstone into blocks. One or more faces were pecked to a relatively smooth surface, giving a "dimpled" effect. This technique continued through the entire period.

Collections of families or clans willing to live together for mutual support and defense lived in these new villages. The houses had thick walls, and some were multistoried. It appears that there were many modifications of walls and houses. Outside-facing doorways on the ground level were few. Some rooms had ladder openings in the ceilings to upper levels, again suggesting a need for defense.

Left: The tallest structure in the park is Square Tower House, which was 86 feet (26 m) high. Originally there were 80 rooms but only 60 rooms and 7 kivas remain.

Right: The impressive size of Far View House and nearby Pipe Shrine House (the smaller ruin) is clearly evident. There are a number of these large communities adjacent to Far View village.

Far View

Visitors to Chapin Mesa have a good opportunity to visit and examine Far View House and several other villages in that vicinity where there are over a dozen ancient sites. The many villages of this complex were constructed in a very favorable location for growing corn, beans, and squash. Although the tree rings found in logs of this period show there were recurring droughts, more rain fell on the upper portion of the mesas, so it was a good place to farm.

Normal winter snowfall at this elevation increased ground moisture, so spring planting could be started before the summer rains began. Living in the Far View House area in winter must have been a real hardship, with deep snows, strong winds, and cold temperatures much of the time. Tremendous quantities of wood would have had to be gathered by late fall if families were to have enough fuel to survive long periods of cold weather. Despite evidence of long occupation, one wonders if the Far View villages were used seasonally rather than all year around.

Cliff Palace in Winter

Heavy snow generally occurs in the Far View area, so it is very likely these sites were only used at times other than winter.

From the size of the Far View villages it is obvious that community involvement was essential to build such large community houses. While there were a number of moderate sized villages built during this period, not everyone lived in them. Many families preferred to live in smaller unit houses, judging from the number that have been found on the mesas. Large villages create benefits but also create problems. If many people live in a concentrated area, the surrounding lands would have to be utilized to their fullest extent if enough food was to be grown. A large population also needed a dependable and adequate water supply. Springs and seeps provided some water, but at Far View the reservoir was the major domestic water supply.

By A.D. 1150 some of the Pueblo people started to move into alcoves under canyon rims to build new homes. The major shift of population from mesa tops took place about A.D. 1200, when construction of the large cliff dwellings began. The reason for this move from mesas into alcoves is not fully understood. One would see the need for some form of protection as most logical, but for over 600 years the people had lived on the mesas. Why now were they to start a new type of village?

The problems of building new houses in alcoves were numerous. The people had to gather stones along the canyon slopes, carry dirt and water to make mortar, and fashion their house arrangements according to the contour of the alcoves. The people had to carry everything they needed over rough terrain. Obviously something created major tension that changed their daily lives.

Cliff Palace

Defense Theory

The major theory for decades was that the Pueblo people were building for defense. If so, who were their enemies? There is currently no evidence of any other people than Pueblo in the immediate area until after the final abandonment of Mesa Verde.

Were the people fighting among themselves because they could no longer grow enough food, or were there social reasons? Unless crop lands were occasionally changed, the soil nutrients would be depleted and more frequent crop failures would occur. When food was scarce, it is likely that some raiding of farm plots occurred. It seems unlikely, however, that this would have caused the change in house location from mesa tops to alcoves.

Because the defense theory has been so prominent, it would be well to consider how villages like Cliff Palace could be defended. The houses were built in large alcoves with overhanging ledges; it would be difficult to drop anything on them. Only a direct assault could be attempted. The steep slope would make it difficult for an enemy to attack. Defenders in the houses could carefully aim their arrows at attackers trying to run uphill with poor footwear over rough terrain. If an attack lasted more than a day, the enemy would have to withdraw to obtain water and food. Water and food stored in the cliff houses would serve the defenders at any time. Perhaps the fear of an enemy was the reason they chose such locations to build their homes, but it seems unlikely. There is also no evidence in burials that shows violence.

Climate Theory

Climatic conditions may have been a serious problem. For example, suppose the entire region experienced a colder than normal period extending for some years. The people could have been trying to survive by building in weather-protected alcoves. One clue to the climate is the tree rings found in logs cut down during that time. Tree growth in a wet season will show as wide rings. The narrow rings of growth show that some seasons were very dry. Suppose the climate cooled off and the average temperatures were much lower. If there were fewer days of sunshine, less cambium growth would be added; the tree ring would be narrow even if there was more moisture. Thus, a narrow growth ring might reflect either a drought condition or a cold period during the normal growing season of a tree.

Cliff Palace is the largest cliff dwelling in the Park. It had 217 rooms and 23 kivas, and it housed about 250 persons. When kivas were roofed over, they became good places for daily activities to take place.

The weakness of the colder climate theory is that there are a number of small one to four-room cliff dwellings built on precarious ledges that afforded little climatic protection. Why the people moved from the mesa into the cliffs may never be known.

While there are any number of differently shaped alcoves in which houses could be built, large ones facing south-southwest were preferred. Winter sunshine warmed them every afternoon when it was not snowing. Cliff dwellings facing south to southwest include Cliff Palace, Square Tower House, Spruce Tree House, Buzzard House, Spring House, Long House, and Mug House.

The topography of the large alcoves was the determining factor in how the houses could be built. In Cliff Palace, for example, the natural floor of the alcove sloped downward, which required considerable filling of areas behind walls to make level sites for rooms. In some sites the people built around large boulders they could not move. In most cases all space was utilized to keep the houses under the protection of the alcove roof.

No springs have been found very close to Cliff Palace. If there were some, they dried up long ago. The nearest dependable spring still flowing is across the canyon below Sun Temple. This would be a long walk just to get water. As much construction as possible probably took place in the spring when melting snows yielded water much closer to home, or when water could be collected from heavy rains.

Spruce Tree House

Spruce Tree House is the third largest village in the Park and one of the best preserved because of the low profile of the alcove. A good spring is located a few hundred feet away.

There are not many good places to climb to the top of the cliffs. Older people must have spent most of their time in the village rather than going to the fields. When trash accumulated, the people threw it over the front slope. From this trash, archeologists have learned a great deal about the inhabitants and what they made and used.

The Pueblo people took pride in their wall construction and shaped sandstone into blocks so houses and doors had square corners.

Forming the sandstone into building blocks or making repairs to the walls was a difficult, time-consuming job.

Spruce Tree House, with its 114 rooms and 8 kivas, housed about 125-150 people.

Nearly all daytime work in the village was carried on in the open courtyards. These probably bristled with activities. Women would grind corn, prepare food, and make baskets and clothing. Men made a variety of tools from wood and stone, sometimes in the courtyard and other times within the kivas. Building a kiva below the surface made good use of the space since the roof above was a work area. In winter the courtyard was about the only snowfree area where youngsters could play.

Above: Doors bordering the courtyard were small, making it easier to keep rooms warm at night or during winter.

Right: Since the Pueblo people did not have cloth to use for door coverings, they frequently used sandstone slabs.

53

Above: Balcony House, with its 45 rooms and 2 kivas, was the most defensible village of its size found at Mesa Verde.
Inset: North end of Balcony House, with its protective wall along the front.

Balcony House

Balcony House, built on a high, easily defended ledge, had only one entry/exit way. It had been carefully fortified so everyone entering or leaving could be controlled by a guard. A great deal of stone and fill material had to be carried into the alcove to level it for house construction. At the north end of the village, a three foot high wall was built along the front to keep small youngsters from toppling over the cliff, but there is no evidence there was one on the south end of the village.

Balcony House faces to the east. In winter it only had a few hours of sunshine before it was in the shadow the rest of the day. Balcony House would have been a very cold place to live. Smoke-covered walls at the rear of the cave suggest fires were probably maintained to keep the people warm. Gathering wood each fall was probably more vital here than in most of the other cliff houses at Mesa Verde. It is interesting to note that one timber found in the entry/exit tunnel dates to A.D. 1278, one of the latest dated timbers used in construction found at Mesa Verde. Was this one of the last groups of people to hold out until they too had to leave?

Balcony House may have been one of the last occupied dwellings at Mesa Verde.

Most floors between upper and lower rooms were made of stringers of juniper, covered with mud, juniper bark, and more mud. These supported considerable weight, and fires could be built on them in upper floors.

Visitors thrill at climbing the ladder into Balcony House.

Everyone who goes through Balcony House has a real appreciation for the ancient Anasazi inhabitants.

Long House on Wetherill Mesa

The second largest ruin in the Park is Long House, located on Wetherill Mesa. As the name implies, it does not have the clustered rooms of Cliff Palace. There seems to be less refinement of building stones, as if the builders did not take as much time to shape the stones as they did in houses on Chapin Mesa.

Above the main village in Long House are two ledges with rooms built on them. Imagine the difficulty of carrying stones and mud up poorly made ladders to utilize the space above! The northern ledge has a wall with many small openings at different angles as if someone was watching village behavior or activities from above. It was reached by a high ladder from a lower roof top.

Dependable springs near Long House were the main source of water. A number of small seeps exist in the back of Long House. Snow, of course, could be melted in winter. Long House, like so many ruins, faces into the winter sunshine, and it was probably a good place to have lived. In our world today we sometimes feel we have "cabin fever" when we can't get out and go somewhere. Imagine how these people felt when there was deep snow on the ground for several months at a time!

About 150 people lived in Long House with its 150 rooms and 21 kivas.

Step House

Step House received its name from the stone steps that were built on the southern slope in prehistoric times as a way to the rim. About thirty or forty Pueblo people lived in the Classic village.

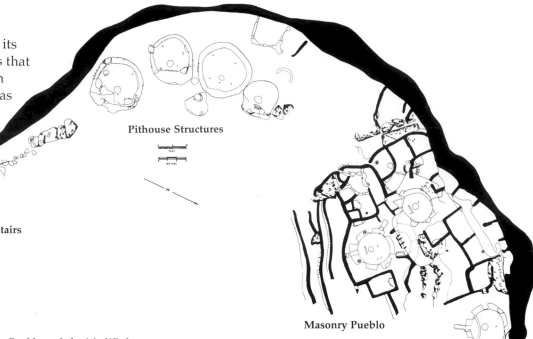

Pithouse Structures

Prehistoric Stairs

Masonry Pueblo

Both Pueblo houses of the Classic Pueblo and the Modified Basketmaker houses are found in Step House alcove.

Mug House

One of the ruins discovered on Wetherill Mesa most rich in artifacts was Mug House. In 1890 when Charles Mason and the Wetherill brothers explored the ruin, they found four or five pottery mugs tied together with string, so they called the site Mug House. The inhabitants apparently specialized in making pottery mugs, as a fairly large number were found here.

Several hundred feet south of Mug House the people built a small water reservoir next to the cliff. This reservoir was much closer than the larger spring in the canyon below.

According to notes of explorer Richard Wetherill, several mugs tied on to a string were found in a ruin. After many mugs were found there, the ruin was given the name Mug House.

Below: Mug House had 94 rooms and 8 kivas. The last improvements took place in A.D. 1277.

Kivas and Social Organization

The ancient Pueblo farmers of Mesa Verde left no written records of their way of life when they abandoned the region about A.D. 1300. They left behind their house remains, pottery, weapons, tools, ornaments, and clothing to be interpreted by those who followed. Scientists studying southwestern archeology have long recognized the similarities between ancient Pueblo sites and existing Pueblo people, their architecture and their general way of life. It is upon such comparisons that archeologists must rely in reaching certain conclusions about how the people lived and what they may have believed.

Among the present western Pueblo people the social structure or organization is based upon clans following a matrilineal line of descent. A clan is normally composed of individuals descended from the same female ancestor. The house belongs to the woman, and when a daughter marries she and her husband often live with the wife's mother or add a room on her house. A house, then, could have a number of rooms if the mother had four or five daughters who married and had families. The husbands of these women do not belong to their wife's clan, but retain their religious affiliation with their mother's clan. The males conduct the religious activities in the kivas of their mother's clan.

These subsurface chambers with their special features serve as a place for religious ritual and religious planning. They are also used as club rooms, a special workshop, or a place of leisure. Women are generally, but not totally excluded from kivas. Men's activities are more closely associated with the kivas and women's with the house proper.

Typical Mesa Verde kiva of the Classic Period. Pueblo Indians have visited Mesa Verde in recent times and have made comments about how clans like to have certain things in their kivas that were present in prehistoric times.

The tension bar of a simple weaving loom was tied down to the floor of this kiva in Long House. Men did the weaving.

Since houses occupied most upper levels, kivas were built on the front and below, often adjoining each other. In one such grouping it is possible to go through connecting tunnels between four kivas without going through a normal overhead entry. In use, the tunnel would permit someone of importance in a special society to enter a kiva at a particular moment for an impressive effect.

Most kivas have some minor construction differences. Kiva orientation was usually determined by the shape of available space in which a kiva could be built. Just as we today have individual ideas of construction, the various clans built their kivas differently than other nearby clans.

With the exception of a few sites, most kivas were constructed to be subsurface. Kivas had a vertical shaft ventilator with a tunnel opening into the kiva to allow air to enter. The deflector prevented a draft on the fire, allowing oxygen to enter the kiva. Smoke went out the overhead entry.

Kivas built below the earth's surface are closer to the Pueblo place of origin and therefore a good place to plan religious activities. Most kivas have a Sipapu (a spirit entrance) to the Four Worlds below, from which the Pueblo people believe they arrived on the earth's surface.

The emphasis on religion at Long House is obvious by the number of rooms that have been modified. Many square or oblong rooms, which were once living rooms, were converted into round kivas. New smaller kivas were often built within larger kivas.

In Long House there is a large rectangular area occupying a central location in the middle of the village. This was a great kiva and dance plaza. Pueblo religion was obviously very important, since the space used for the big kiva could have been used for houses. The great kiva has a large recessed stone-lined firepit, bordered on each side by another oblong recessed depression that may have served as a foot drum when used during ceremonial or secular activities. Animal hides were probably stretched across these openings to serve as drum heads. This is the largest great kiva in the Park, but another oblong kiva that probably served the same function is found in Fewkes Canyon on the Mesa Top Drive on Chapin Mesa.

The oblong-shaped areas in Long House and in Fewkes Canyon below Sun Temple were large kivas with dance plazas for public ceremonies.

The great kiva at Fire Temple, a name applied by Dr. Jesse Fewkes, has painted pictures of men, animals, plants, and geometric designs. These paintings are similar to types found in some present Hopi ceremonial rooms relating to the "New Fire" ceremonials, according to Dr. Fewkes. Such comparisons help archeologists determine relationships between the ancient and present Indians of the Southwest.

Dances, a form of visual prayer, frequently occurred in villages for many different purposes.

Above: Farmers used digging sticks to plant corn. As the crops matured, it was important to tend the fields and keep birds and animals away.

Below: Prehistoric corn, beans, and squash specimens found in ruins at Mesa Verde.

Farming

Pueblo life revolved around farming activities, which were very important for survival. There is no way of knowing how long farmers used the same plot in growing corn, beans, and squash. It is suspected that they noticed that corn planted on new land grew taller than on reused land. There was a never-ending effort to expand croplands by cutting or burning trees to open new areas.

After a long winter when food supplies were depleted, the need to plant corn promptly would be a high priority. Corn was planted five or six inches (13 or 15 cm) deep. Modern Hopi (Pueblo) Indians form a small depression where the corn is planted with a circle of dirt piled around it so it can collect and hold any rain that might fall. It is possible that the same technique was used in ancient times too. The practice of building check dam farming plots or terraces in natural drainage areas continued.

Inset: Navajo Indian corn was selected for a crop experiment, because prehistoric corn will not germinate.

Metate corn grinders and mano handstones were made by the hundreds. Digging sticks were a very common work tool.

There are no permanent streams at Mesa Verde, so the Indians had to depend upon dry-land farming techniques. To find out how successful this could be, one of the early archeologists working in the Park, Dr. Jesse W. Fewkes, cleared a plot of forest and planted corn. He allowed the summer rains to water it, and the crop was completely successful. He continued the experiment each year during his stay, and the Park continued it until 1973. In all 55 years of the experiment there were only three crop failures: 1924, 1934, and 1972, when no moisture fell until the growing season was over.

Beans were important to the Pueblo people too. The violet-striped bean was the most common. A climbing type, it could be grown on some of the terraces near the villages or interspersed with the corn. While visiting Long House, some Hopi Indians made the comment that the terraces there

would be a good place for beans, as temperatures would remain warmer at night. Squash, not as susceptible to cold temperatures, was grown in many places. After harvest, ears of corn had to be saved as seed for the next season. Sometimes corn was tied together and hung on rungs in the wall or stacked in storage areas for more immediate use. Some storage rooms were sealed to keep rodents from eating or damaging the corn.

Undoubtedly many native plants were utilized for food or medicine. One method archeologists use to find out which plants may have been eaten is to grind up human feces and examine the material under a microscope. One of the more common plants eaten in the springtime was the Rocky Mountain bee plant. All of the native plants that grow here today also grew in prehistoric times.

Fine examples of Classic Mesa Verde pottery.

Mesa Verde pottery reached its peak of sophistication in form and beauty.

Pottery of the Classic Pueblo Period

The pottery of this period is known for its clear, black geometric designs on a grayish-white background. Although not as common, there are some expressions of animals, birds, and human forms on the pottery. Pottery was hand-painted with a remarkable sense of design balance. Often bowl interiors had elaborate designs. The dot pattern on vessel rims is a typical Classic trait. Kiva storage jars are some of the finest examples of perfect shape, design, and finish. Small, medium, and large mugs found almost everywhere in Classic Pueblo sites show the fine artistic skill of the potters. Large jars with small necks, pitchers, ladles, and shallow bowls were very common. Corrugated vessels, common through all Pueblo periods, continued to serve as cooking and storage jars. Sometimes clay scrolls were applied to these jars. One cannot help but admire the shapes, designs, and workmanship of the ancient potters of Mesa Verde.

Corrugated vessels served as cooking and storage jars.

A narrow groove was ground into a granite or igneous rock after it was shaped into an ax so that a handle could be hafted to it.

The ancient Anasazi were Stone Age people and did not have metal.

Stone Tools

Some visitors to Mesa Verde find it hard to believe the ancient Anasazi were Stone Age people and did not have metal. The problem of making tools at Mesa Verde was complicated because most of the rock is soft sandstone and not suitable for making good tools. Cutting tools had to be made from harder rock. Trips were made to the Mancos River or distant mountains to find good rock. When one considers that it takes some sort of tool to make almost anything, the importance of tools seems more real.

The evolution of architecture from Modified Basketmaker times to the Classic Pueblo period required the use of many hundreds of stone axes to cut timbers and to shape wood needed in construction. These were often made in different shapes, showing that they functioned for specific needs. Some had right angle notches, and some were partially or fully grooved for hafting onto a handle. Some axes were finely polished, while others were rough.

Stone bladed knives were used to make clothing, to cut animal hides and plants, and to make other tools. Such knives were often hafted to wooden handles to make them easier to use. Drills served many uses, but there were not a great number of projectile points made. Wooden arrow shaft ends were fire-hardened in place of a stone point. Hundreds of hammerstones used in house construction have been found.

To make a mano for grinding corn, nuts, and plant foods on a metate, the rough stone was shaped so it had a relatively flat surface. Large boulders, usually in villages, were a favorite site for shaping manos and stone axes to make them more functional. Archeologists are studying grooves in Step House.

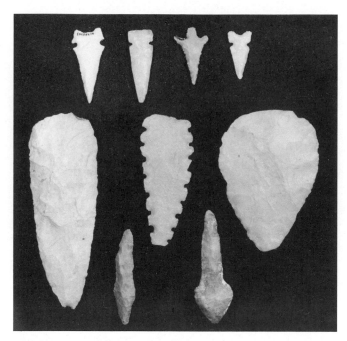

Blade knives, drills, and projectile points.

Bone

In addition to stone tools, bones of animals were fashioned into many useful items. Larger game animal bones were often split and made into awls or flesh scrapers. Women used awls in making clothing and for making holes in hides. Some awls were used in weaving as loom tools. Bones from turkeys, mule deer, bighorn sheep, and rabbits were preferred.

These awls, scrapers, and fleshers are typical bone tools. The tubular bone necklace was found in Mug House.

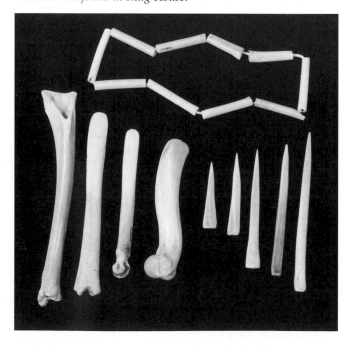

Ornaments and Trade

Ornaments and items of personal adornment are always interesting and are usually highly treasured by their owners. Ornaments of all types have been found in all periods of Pueblo habitation at Mesa Verde, but perhaps not in the quantity one might imagine. It is suspected that since most recovered ornaments are small, the people may have taken much of their jewelry with them. A few necklaces that have been found in burials show the variety of ornaments made.

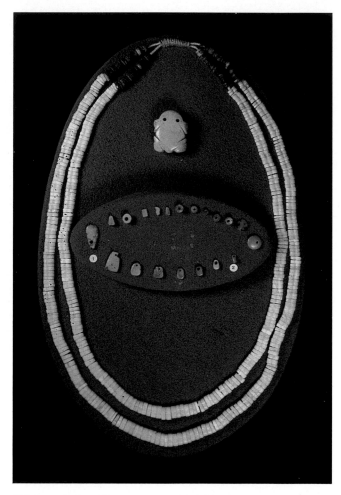

This beautiful necklace was made of shells from the Pacific Ocean area.

Prehistoric Trading

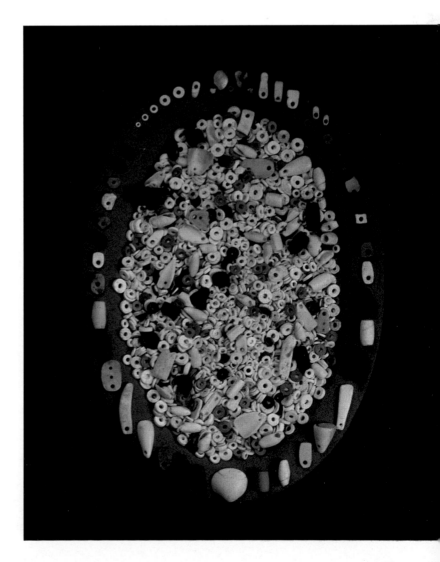

Map labels: Nevada, Utah, Colorado, California, Arizona, New Mexico, MESA VERDE, Pacific Ocean, TURQUOISE, OBSIDIAN, SHELL ORNAMENTS, SALT, ARGILLITE, RED POTTERY, LIGNITE, TURQUOISE, COTTON CLOTH, STEATITE, ABALONE, CONUS, GLYCYMERIS, CARDIUM, TURITELLA

A figure called Kokopelli (from Zuni-Hopi dialects) shows up as a design element in petroglyphs and on pottery from A.D. 700 to A.D. 1600 throughout the Southwest. Whether he was a trader with a pack on his back or a humpbacked individual caused by physical deforminty has never fully been determined.

Commerce between people of the Southwest has continued for over a thousand years, right up to present times.

Many local wood, stone, and bone resources were fashioned into useful tools, but some of these materials did not lend themselves to making ornaments. When the Pueblo Indians traveled away from Mesa Verde and came into contact with others, they often brought back new and attractive items, which created a great demand for trading. Having to walk long distances through dry, semi-arid country was apparently no barrier to movement. Most trade routes were established along areas where springs, waterholes, or potholes were known to exist.

Turquoise was traded from areas in New Mexico and Arizona and was highly prized. Ocean shells in a variety of shapes came from the Pacific Ocean and the Baja Gulf. Other items traded included salt, argillite (a red stone that looks like pipestone) for making pendants and little animal figures, and red pottery. Even some cotton came from as far away as southern Arizona, and in some Anasazi areas, copper bells have been found.

The Mesa Verde people may have traded special pieces of pottery, piñon nuts, animal skins, jet and lignite (forms of coal), and even corn. One would expect that both raw materials and finished beads were commonly traded.

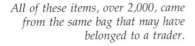

All of these items, over 2,000, came from the same bag that may have belonged to a trader.

Summer Clothing

Women wore a small cotton apron for body covering, but little is known about men's clothing.

Winter Clothing

Turkey-feather blankets and robes were probably common. Tanned animal hides were used and perhaps some cotton cloth.

Clothing

Many thousands of artifacts have been found here, but articles of clothing are nearly non-existent. This is because the people wore little clothing, and the clothing they did wear was used until it was no longer wearable. Clothing made of plant material had the tendency to decay rapidly when it was discarded. Finding hundreds of sandals or their fragments gives the impression that footwear was a very important need.

These people lived outdoors all their lives and were better acclimated to lower temperatures than we could tolerate today.

The Importance of the Yucca

Of all the native plants growing at Mesa Verde, one plant was most important — the yucca. It grows nearly everywhere in the area except along the high escarpment. This drought-resistant plant was available as a resource to make clothing, sandals, blankets, snares, baskets, and cordage for sewing, as well as for food and soap. The sharp barbs on the leaves were used as needles and as paint brushes for painting pottery.

The wide leaf yucca is not only beautiful, but was a tremendous resource for making many things.

Health

The Pueblo people did not look forward to winter, for those in poor health would suffer, and some might die. The old people and babies were most susceptible to the damp and cold. With much snow on the ground, sanitation was surely a problem. Some of the back rooms were used as bathrooms. Such use would help foster disease. Skeletal remains show that many individuals over 29 years of age had degenerative arthritis, especially along the spinal column. Abnormalities were not uncommon. Some bone fractures have been noted, but fewer than one might expect in the canyon topography the people called home.

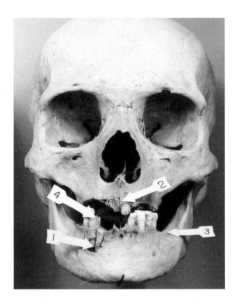

Dental problems appear to have been very common among the population.

1. Abscess
2. Misalignment
3. Resorption
4. Attrition

Offerings buried with the deceased reveal the belief that they would need certain items in the other world they were entering.

While there were many dental problems, the Pueblo people had fewer cavities than most Americans. There was a marked attrition (worn down teeth) caused by the grit in corn meal ground on metates. Tartar shows on teeth, and pyorrhea was common.

When a communicable disease swept any village there was a good possibility that many could die. There was an ever-present danger that someone might fall from a cliff. If people died in winter, the survivors had only two choices in handling the deceased: they could bury bodies in the trash dump or in abandoned rooms at the rear of the village. The trash dump in front of the village was about the only place soft enough to dig a grave in winter. This method of disposal was not a disrespectful act but a practical solution to an immediate problem. No graveyards have been found. Perhaps some were buried along canyon slopes that have since eroded away. Some were buried in cracks in the cliff and some under floors. Just over 200 burials have been found so far in excavations, which is a small percentage when one considers that as many as 5,000 people lived here during Classic Pueblo times.

From burials, anthropologists have been able to determine the age, sex, and physical well-being of the ancient inhabitants. Men averaged about 5 feet 4 inches (163 cm), and women were slightly shorter. Most people were of slight stature and few lived much beyond 40 years. By the mid-1200s more women were dying between the ages of 20 and 25; men were living to between 31 and 35 years. These conditions were directly attributable to lack of adaptation to changing environmental conditions.

Petroglyphs & Pictographs

The sandstone cliffs at Mesa Verde were good places to peck or carve designs or to paint upon, yet there is little of this art form in the area. Most of the painted pictographs are designs painted upon walls of rooms or in weather-sheltered places. There may have been many more wall paintings, but little has survived the erosion of seven centuries since the Pueblo departed.

About a mile and one-half (2 km) south of the Museum is the largest display of petroglyphs found in the Park. Interpretation of the elements is as varied as the mind of the viewer allows. Geometric designs, plants, and a few animal figures are common. One Hopi visitor feels that one design is a clan symbol that may be ancestral Hopi. Elsewhere in the Park there are a few other isolated designs. In Step House there are some petroglyphs on a boulder. It is hard to understand why so few forms of rock art are found at Mesa Verde unless the inhabitants had social or other restrictions on them. They may have expressed themselves more in their pottery.

Top Left: This elaborate wall painting can be seen in the four-story dwelling in Cliff Palace. Red ochre and hematite were used to make paint for wall paintings.

Inset: An artist's conception of a petroglyph being pecked into the cliff.

Right: At Petroglyph Point a variety of human, animal, and geometric designs were carved into the cliff to depict special significance.

The Abandonment of Mesa Verde

We have seen the growth of the Anasazi from the hunting-gathering culture of the Basketmakers to the rather sophisticated society of the Classic Period. Despite improvements in their architecture and their general technology, all was not going well. For centuries the Pueblo people had been able to cope with droughts numbering from 10 to 12 a century and grow sufficient crops to survive. They had learned that small farming plots behind check dams increased the food supply when crops elsewhere were marginal. They had found that small farming plots on the northeast sides of the mesas remained moist longer than others and also produced better corn, beans, and squash. For many centuries the Pueblo farmers had farmed the mesa tops, continually cutting or burning away the forest to open new land for crops. As more and more fields were abandoned from lack of soil nutrients, the dry soils began to blow away or to wash rapidly into the canyons during sudden downpours. It is entirely possible that this condition was occurring at the same time the people were seeking the large alcoves in the cliffs to build their new homes.

Rainfall, so important to agriculture, was more borderline than abundant, resulting in poor crop production. Fewer animals were on the mesas to be hunted, and less food was available to a people already having problems from over-population. Hungry people perhaps began to fight and quarrel, and more and more raiding of fields could have occurred as the people sought to obtain food.

Perhaps the food problem was one reason so many rooms in Long House were converted to kivas, indicating more clan emphasis on religion. On Chapin Mesa a large ceremonial structure, Sun Temple, was being constructed on a prominent point across from Cliff Palace. Unlike most mesa-top structures, it did not appear to be a village, but apparently was of community importance. This was possibly a place where the rain gods might be appeased in the hope that more rain would fall. It could not have been constructed without the aid of the community, and it seems to have been carefully planned, although never completed. Archeologists can only speculate on how it was to be used, but visiting Pueblo people say it was of ceremonial significance.

Spectacularly located, Sun Temple was a ceremonial center for the large cluster of villages in the vicinity.

In A.D. *1273*
it stopped raining...

The Abandonment of Mesa Verde

The population had reached numbers that demanded more food than marginal farmlands could produce. Even though a drought-resistant strain of maize was being used, it could not replace the lack of soil fertility. The stonework in some post A.D. 1250 dwellings shows less refinement and seemingly was less important to the builders. The inability of the Pueblos to adapt to their problems was a major factor in the decline of the society. More and more people were dying, though there is no evidence of hostile enemy people having moved into the area.

In A.D. 1273 the rain stopped. The drought continued until A.D. 1285. This was the final blow that broke the Pueblos' ability to hold out longer. More and more people started to leave, taking what few treasured items they could carry. Archeological evidence shows they moved south into New Mexico and northern Arizona, where some of the present Pueblo people live. Some Acoma (Pueblo) people feel their ancestors may have come from Mesa Verde, as do some Hopi in Arizona. Many anthropologists think the Keres-speaking Pueblos of New Mexico are the descendants of the ancient Anasazi of Mesa Verde.

It appears today that environmental destruction and over-population, coupled with climatic changes, ended the 700-year occupation of Mesa Verde by the ancient Pueblo peoples.

Unable to adapt to harsh environmental conditions and very little rainfall, the discouraged ancient farmers started leaving Mesa Verde for a better place to live.

Mesa Verde has the distinction of beginning the first campfire programs and museum in the National Park Service. These were started by Dr. Jesse Fewkes, an archeologist for the Smithsonian Institituion.

... in front of them, through the falling snow, appeared a stone city three stories high in places.

HISTORY OF MESA VERDE NATIONAL PARK

Two Story Cliff House by William Henry Jackson, 1874.

JUST WHO REALLY DISCOVERED the fabulous cliff dwellings of Mesa Verde may never be known. History shows that Franciscan Friars Dominguez and Escalante, seeking a route from Santa Fe to Monterey in California, passed just north of Mesa Verde in August of 1776 without actually exploring the mesas or canyons. In 1829, Antonio Armijo, also from Santa Fe, passed Mesa Verde but did not report seeing any large cliff dwellings. In 1859, Professor John S. Newberry, a geologist with the Macomb Expedition, was curious about what was on top of the high escarpment, so he climbed it. In his notes, he wrote about how beautiful the view was from Mesa Verde. He, like the others who had passed earlier, did not explore the distant canyons, as this was not the goal of the expedition. The descriptive name "Mesa Verde" means "green table" in Spanish. We do not know who gave it that name, but it was most likely the early Spanish explorers. Apparently the name was commonly known at the time the Macomb Expedition passed by the mesa.

The discovery of gold and silver in the Rocky Mountains brought many people into the eastern part of Colorado, where Ute Indians still roamed. The new settlers claimed the land and thought the Utes should be assigned specific areas west of the mountains. Congress signed a treaty in 1868 which gave the Utes most of the land west of the Continental Divide. Gold and silver was then discovered west of the mountains. As a result, the Ute Treaty was modified in 1873, giving the Utes a strip of land about 15 miles (24 km) deep into Colorado along the New Mexico boundary line in southwest Colorado. Geographically, this included much of Mesa Verde, with the exception of the northern escarpment.

The Utes were not particularly friendly at this time, so most travelers avoided going onto Ute lands. The Utes themselves did not make much use of the mesas and canyons, as they feared the spirits of the departed ancient ones.

It remained for a famous photographer to first record the cliff dwellings on film. This was William Henry Jackson, who had photographed much of the Yellowstone country several years earlier, submitting his photos as part of the package of recommendations to Congress to make that area a national park. In 1874, Jackson was in charge of the Photographic Division of the U.S. Geological and Geographic Survey of the Territories and was recording mining activities in the Silverton district. During his assignment, he ran across a friend named Tom Cooper, who was working several mining claims in the La Plata Mountains southwest of Silverton. Cooper told Jackson and his party of seven that one of the men at the mines, a man named Captain Moss, had told him of canyons at Mesa Verde with cliff dwellings in them. (It is entirely probable that an early prospector was the first non-Indian to see some of the cliff dwellings, which were still officially undiscovered.)

Left: In 1917 the ranger station near headquarters was converted to a small museum with photos and some artifacts. It was the first museum established in a national park.

The 1874 Jackson Party.

Impressed with the story, Jackson decided to investigate. Moss, who spoke the Ute language, agreed to guide them through the region since most of Mancos Canyon was on Ute lands. In September, the Jackson party proceeded down Mancos Canyon.

The first night out, as the party was finishing its evening meal, Jackson tells of kidding one young man named Steve about having to carry equipment up to a ruin to photograph it. When Steve asked, "Where?" Captain Moss pointed up and said, "Right up there!" Steve strained his eyes and then said, "Yes, I can see it!" Much to the surprise of everyone, there was a ruin.

Everyone rushed to climb to it. Only Jackson and party member Ingersoll managed to actually reach the ruin, built high into the vertical cliff about a hundred feet (30 m) from the mesa top. As Jackson and Ingersoll looked about, Jackson later expressed his feelings by writing, "From this height we had a glorious view over the surrounding canyon walls, while far below our campfire glimmered in the deepening shadows like a far away little red star." The next morning they returned to the ruin, photographed it, and gave it

the name "Two Story Cliff House." Before they left the canyon, they explored another ruin.

In 1875, William H. Holmes visited the ruin known as Sixteen Window House (on the Ute Reservation), collecting a few pieces of pottery that he later sent to the National Museum. Holmes recorded a number of Indian ruins in southwestern Colorado, but apparently did not visit some of the larger ones in what is now the Park.

In 1882, Virginia Donaghe McClurg, a correspondent for the *New York Graphic*, arrived in Durango to investigate lost cities of the prehistoric Indians of the Southwest. Due to an uprising by the Ute Indians, she left, returning again in 1885. Able then to explore only a few small ruins, her next effort was in 1886 when she hired a guide and a photographer. With two pack animals, they set out to explore some of the lower canyons that emptied into the Mancos River. Her small expedition is credited with locating Three Tiered House and Echo Cliff House. Her most important exploration was of Brownstone Front located by her companion Cassius Viets. This ruin, now called Balcony House, was to become an important incentive to Virginia McClurg in her future effort to preserve the cliff dwellings.

Al, Win, Richard, Clayton, and John Wetherill

The Wetherills

In 1881, the Quaker family of Benjamin K. Wetherill settled about three miles (5 km) southwest of the very small town of Mancos. Within a year the local newspaper was praising the "Alamo Ranch," as it was called, for the fine condition of its acreage. Benjamin and his five sons had worked hard developing the ranch and its buildings. They were frequently visited by Ute Indians stopping by for food or even medical aid. The Wetherills always helped them and were considered friends even when there were problems between the Utes and other ranchers.

As Benjamin and his five sons increased their acreage and cattle herds, they had to have a winter

range for the cattle. The Mancos Valley received considerable snow. The Mancos River flowed south toward lower elevations, so the Wetherills drove their cattle down to the vicinity of Johnson Canyon (on the present Ute Mountain Ute Reservation) for winter forage. A cabin was built in 1884 or 1885 to serve as winter camp.

During their stay at the winter camp, boredom was the rule. Richard and Al often rode off to explore nearby mesas and canyons for ruins. They found a number of cliff dwellings. Brother-in-law Charles Mason sometimes rode with them when he was at the winter camp. One day, while Richard was looking up the mouth of Cliff Canyon, a Ute named Acowitz approached him and after some deliberation said, "Deep in that canyon and near its head are many houses of the old people — the Ancient Ones. One of those houses, high, high in the rocks, is bigger than all the others. Utes never go there, it is a sacred place." Although Richard tried to learn more, Acowitz would say no more.

Inset: Acowitz
Below: Cliff Palace as it was seen in 1891.

On December 18, 1888, Richard Wetherill and Charles Mason were riding across the mesas looking for stray cattle.

A heavy snow storm blurred the distant view. Knowing nearby cliffs might be closer than expected, Richard and Charles dismounted and walked over to a point where they could get their perspective. In utter astonishment they gazed at the scene below. Across the canyon, through the falling snow, appeared a stone city three stories high in places. Forgetting the strays, they clambered along the cliff until they could find a way down the steep face. Finally they lashed several tree trunks together and climbed down and worked their way to Cliff Palace.

After several hours of exploring the ruin, they decided to return to the canyon rim separately and see if they could find anything more. Richard was lucky and found Spruce Tree House, but Charles found nothing. They camped overnight.

The next morning, in an attempt to return to Spruce Tree House, they drifted south and came across Square Tower House. Finding no other ruins that day, they returned to their winter cabin in Johnson Canyon. For Richard it was the start of a life-long effort to find more ruins, a search that eventually took him into Utah and New Mexico.

In succeeding years, the Wetherills collected thousands of artifacts from the ruins at Mesa Verde. Richard started to record where the items came from. His first large collection was sold to The Colorado State Historical Society after attempts at lecturing to spark the interest of others failed. Their second collection was sold to the C.D. Hazard and Jay Smith Exploring Company of Jackson Park, Illinois, who exhibited it in the 1893 Chicago World's Fair. After the fair was over, the collection was shipped to the University of Pennsylvania; Mrs. Phoebe H. Hearst purchased the items for that institution. The Wetherills' last collection was displayed in the Colorado exhibits of the Chicago Fair and was then purchased by the Colorado State Museum in Denver.

The Wetherills served as guides for hundreds of visitors at Mesa Verde, including a newspaper reporter named Frederick Chapin. After visiting Mesa Verde, Chapin wrote articles about the Wetherills' efforts. The Wetherills named the mesa, on which Spruce Tree House stands, "Chapin" in his honor.

While some persons have criticized the Wetherills, they sold their collections primarily to museums, where many of the artifacts can still be seen today. Richard and his family ultimately moved to Chaco Canyon in New Mexico, where Richard continued his search for ruins.

John (left) and Richard Wetherill in Spruce Tree House ruin.

The removal of artifacts from prehistoric ruins by early explorers and visitors was a serious problem On a visit to the area about 1904, George Beam photographed one such collection.

Gustaf Nordenskiöld

Two and a half years after Richard Wetherill and Charles Mason reported seeing Cliff Palace, a buggy pulled by a pair of horses arrived at the Benjamin Wetherill Ranch. It was carrying a gentleman from Sweden who came to see the sights around Mancos. The man was Gustaf Nordenskiöld. Only 23 years old, he was touring the United States seeking a dry, warm climate to ease the tuberculosis he had contracted in Finland. He had heard of some Indian dwellings in southwestern Colorado from a friend living in Denver, so he came to see for himself. He had no idea there were so many ruins; instead of staying a week as he planned, he spent the summer and autumn excavating ruins at nearby Mesa Verde. Others were collecting artifacts, and since there were no laws prohibiting this, he began a collection also.

Although not trained in archeology, Nordenskiöld was familiar with scientific methods. His father was a famous arctic explorer and mineralogist; other relatives were involved in science, too. Nordenskiöld himself had served on a scientific expedition. His attitude, his ability, and his resultant book were to mark his short stay at Mesa Verde.

Gustaf Nordenskiöld

Balcony House, as photographed in 1891 by Nordenskiöld.

In his book, "The Cliff Dwellers of the Mesa Verde," published in 1893 upon his return to Sweden, Nordenskiöld describes his explorations and investigations. To avoid the steep escarpment he was taken down the Mancos Canyon by the Wetherills until they came to the mouth of Soda Canyon. They proceeded up-canyon until they reached the cliff dwellings. His reference to various mesas or canyons shows that most had been "named" in the two preceding years; these names remain the same today and help us to follow his writings.

After visiting a few ruins, Nordenskiöld wrote home and had his camera sent so he could record what he was seeing. The photographs he took were excellent; they record how many of the ruins looked within the first three years following discovery. It is remarkable that the ruins have survived so well, considering all the explorations that took place before the area was established as a national park in 1906. A small collection of his photographs can be seen in the Chapin Mesa Archeological Museum. He made over 150 photographs in all.

Above: Balcony House photographed by Nordenskiöld in 1891.

Below: Spruce Tree House in 1891.

Some of the 615 artifacts collected by Nordenskiöld.

Beginning July 14, 1891, Nordenskiöld and John Wetherill began searching Long House Ruin (on Wetherill Mesa) while operating out of a camp about 1.8 miles (3 km) to the north. Nordenskiöld, incidentally, named the mesa after the Wetherills, a name that entices visitors to that far western portion of the Park. Long House was so big and had so much fallen rock that after four weeks of trying to excavate, Nordenskiöld decided to move south to another ruin they called Kodak House. Rather than carry his camera back and forth to Wetherill Mesa from Chapin Mesa, Nordenskiöld stored his camera in this dwelling while working ruins on the western side of the area. After working in Kodak House and several nearby ruins, the camp was moved back up the mesa a short distance from Mug House. This campsite has been located at the junction of the parking area, about a mile (2 km) north of Long House. After partially investigating Mug House, Nordenskiöld visited nearby Step House, where he became interested in a number of burials. Many turkey droppings were found in both ruins, and he speculated that turkeys were commonly used by the ancient people in making turkey-feather blankets. When Step House was partially excavated, Nordenskiöld returned to work in Spruce Tree House.

By early September, Nordenskiöld had collected and sent hundreds of specimens by pack team to Mancos, where they were put on the train and shipped to Durango. The arrival of so many specimens caused a public uproar. Although authorities called Nordenskiöld to Durango to discuss the matter, nothing came of it. The specimens were shipped on to Sweden. It was this removal of specimens that incited the first efforts to protect the archeological resources of Mesa Verde.

Nordenskiöld was a very perceptive young man. During a short several months he covered a vast amount of physical terrain, testing and excavating in a sizeable number of ruins. He observed that there were distinct types of pottery and described each of them in his book. He also gave good descriptions of the tools, implements, and various artifacts he found.

For years there was a clamor that the federal government should arrange to have the Nordenskiöld collection returned to Mesa Verde. A National Park Service archeologist went to the National Museum in Helsinki, Finland, where the collection had been donated and stored. He carefully examined and photographed the artifacts. It was decided that the Service has similar artifacts to those in the collection, and because it was in a national museum, it should remain there.

*The arrival of so many
specimens caused a
public uproar.
It was the removal of
specimens that incited the
first efforts to protect the
archeological resources
of Mesa Verde.*

Virginia McClurg Returns

From 1887 to 1906, Virginia McClurg engaged
in a continuous political campaign to inform the
American public and members of Congress of the
need to preserve the cliff dwellings of Mesa Verde.
She toured the country giving speeches and
decrying the wanton destruction of ancient walls
by treasure-seekers who were carrying off artifacts
to sell. Her effort was intensified by writing poems
that were published in many prominent
magazines. She enlisted the aid of the Federation of
Womens Clubs and gained the support of over
250,000 women. Eventually she formed the
Colorado Cliff Dwellers Association whose
statement of purpose was as follows:

> The object of this Association shall be in the
> restoration and preservation of the cliff and
> Pueblo ruins in the State of Colorado; the
> dissemination of knowledge concerning these
> prehistoric peoples; the collection of relics;
> and the acquiring of such property as is
> necessary to attain such objects.

Mrs. McClurg succeeded in negotiating with
the Weminuche Ute Chief Ignacio for the ruins to
be protected while the Utes still retained grazing
rights to the land. This arrangement, which
eventually was ratified by Congress in 1901,
allowed the Colorado Cliff Dwellers Association to
control the ruins. In return, the Utes received $300
a year.

Virginia McClurg, having worked with
members of Congress since 1894, made repeated
unsuccessful attempts to have bills passed in the
interest of Mesa Verde. She continued her efforts,
lecturing in Europe and speaking to scientific
institutions and to a variety of dignitaries in this
country as well. Eventually, total support

Virginia McClurg

*On June 29, 1906,
President Theodore
Roosevelt signed the
bill creating Mesa Verde
National Park.*

was gained, and Congressional action appeared
imminent when it was discovered that the major
ruins were not in the proposed land withdrawal for
the Park. The bill was promptly amended to
include any ruins within five miles (8 km) of the
proposed park. On June 23, the bill passed, and on
June 29, 1906, President Theodore Roosevelt signed
the bill creating Mesa Verde National Park.

Prior to 1913, it took visitors three days to make a round trip visit to the Park from Mancos by pack train.

The process had taken 24 years. The cliff dwellings of Mesa Verde had finally received permanent protection, but just before this was realized, Virginia McClurg decided the area should be a *state* park. The Cliff Dwellers Association could then have direct control.

The first wagon reached Park headquarters on July 13, 1913, when the entrance road was completed.

Lucy Peabody

On May 28, 1914, the first automobiles entered Mesa Verde. A caravan of six cars, three shown here, made the round trip from Mancos to the Park in one day — a memorable event.

This change of heart, just several months before the creation of the Park, split the association into state and federal factions. Leader of the National Park idea, Lucy Peabody, having worked in Washington, was able to exert more political influence than Mrs. McClurg. She moved to Colorado to continue the fight for the National Park. Both women are to be praised for their lengthy and successful endeavors that led to the establishment of Mesa Verde National Park. The nation is indebted to both for their foresight.

As this 1925 photo shows, the famous Knife Edge Road held certain terrors for early park visitors. Though eventualy improved and surfaced, it was abandoned in 1957 when the new tunnel was completed.

National Park & Park Service

Superintendent Jesse Nusbaum started the first regular interpretive services that have continued to this day.

Superintendent Jesse Nusbaum served as Park Superintendent from 1921 to 1931 and again from 1936 to 1939. Later he became Senior Archeologist for the National Park Service until his retirement.

The amendment to include ruins within five miles (8 km) of the Park was vague, and it created problems. In 1908, when the Ute Indians expressed the desire to secure the Ute Mountain tract, new negotiations were started. The Ute Mountain tract was part of the Montezuma National Forest southwest of Cortez. It contained no marketable timber and the land within the five-mile (8 km) zone near the Park was rough, arid, and of little benefit to the Indians. This tract, however, contained the largest and most important cliff dwellings. After several problems were worked out, an agreement was submitted to Congress on January 22, 1913. The agreement gave the Park an additional 24,500 acres (9915 ha) in exchange for 30,240 acres (12238 ha) of Ute Mountain received by the Indians.

The National Park Service was not established until 1916. Therefore, the first Superintendent of Mesa Verde was appointed by the Ute Indian Agency to administer the new area.

During the first years there were a number of superintendents. Inaccessibility of the ruins necessitated improving the horse trail and building a road for Park visitors. One portion known as the Knife Edge was particularly bad. Slides frequently covered portions of it, or sections of the road sank and slipped downhill. In 1957 the tunnel route was constructed to replace the Knife Edge Road.

Mesa Verde has the distinction of beginning the first campfire programs in the National Park Service. These were started in 1915 by Dr. Jesse Walter Fewkes, who was doing archeological work in the Park for the Smithsonian Institution. In 1917 the ranger station was rehabilitated as a museum. This was another first for the Service. Superintendent Jesse Nusbaum started the first regular interpretive services, with Park rangers conducting guided tours through the ruins, interpreting artifacts in the museum, and giving campfire programs, the beginning of interpretive programs that have continued to this day.

The style of architecture adopted by the Corps, contemporary for this area and the mesa environment, was initially designed by Superintendent Nusbaum and his wife for the house they lived in.

The Civilian Conservation Corps - "The CCC Boys"

Once water sources were developed at Spruce Tree spring, the Park headquarters area began to take on a more permanent form. Under the Emergency Works Program of the federal government, several Civilian Conservation Corps camps were built in 1934 when the first CCC enrollees arrived. The first camp was in Prater Canyon (the first canyon west of the tunnel), and one was built a mile north of present headquarters later in the year. Company 861 had 148 persons, and Company 1843 had 140 members.

The enrollees of the CCC built 21 housekeeping cabins and the roads near headquarters.

They put in curbing of quarried stone, walks, trails, a campground, and telephone lines, as well as some of the water system and plumbing. They also quarried stone and helped to build some of the present stone structures that so attractively dot the landscape. Superintendent Nusbaum and his wife designed the house they lived in, and their style of architecture was adopted by the Corps. This style was contemporary in this area and the mesa environment. The CCC made furniture, some of which is still in everyday use at the museum. The majority of the young men in the two companies were from towns in Colorado, with a few from surrounding states.

Between 1921 and 1925 Mrs. Stella M. Leviston of San Francisco and John D. Rockefeller, Jr. each donated $5,000 that was used to make major improvements on the Park museum.

Above: During the period of the depression in the 1930s, the Public Works Administration and the Civilian Conservation Corps also added to the park museum structure. It was completed in 1936 (photo 1935).

Upper Right: Chapin Mesa Archeological Museum in winter.

Right: Car caravans of visitors were guided to the mesa-top ruins and cliff dwellings by park rangers, who also gave museum and campfire programs. Notice the rangers' uniforms in this 1934 photograph.

For over three decades thousands of visitors stayed at Spruce Tree Lodge before new accommodations were built at Far View.

Accommodations

On a high point of the ridge four miles (6 km) north of the archeological museum is the Park's Far View Visitor Center. Though public information and visitor orientation are its primary functions, the display area contains outstanding examples of the crafts of the historic Indians of the American Southwest. Here, visitors can see beautiful items made by the Pueblo, Ute, Navajo, Pima, O'odham, and Apache Indians.

From Far View one can see Shiprock, an old volcanic plug, as well as the general area where the states of Colorado, Utah, Arizona, and New Mexico come together at a common point.

Once the ruins of Mesa Verde became known, more and more people wanted to see them. The immediate problem was how to accommodate visitors, as it took nearly three days to make a round trip from Mancos. Congress, recognizing the problem, authorized concessions to provide such services; the first began to operate on March 21, 1911, as a tent camp. Visitors paid seventy-five cents for a meal and fifty cents for a place to sleep overnight. In the following years all services improved. The Denver and Rio Grande Railroad had a subsidiary company called the Mesa Verde Park Company

that operated the concession until June 10, 1937, when it was sold to Ansel Hall, former Chief of the Field Division of Museums and Education for the National Park Service. Mr. Hall continued to operate the concession, the Mesa Verde Company as it is still known, until his death. Members of his immediate family operated and expanded it until 1977, when it was purchased by the ARA Corporation. Their modern accommodations at Far View and other facilities at Morefield Village and Spruce Tree provide a variety of fine services to the visiting public.

William Henry Jackson did not explore the many canyons of Mesa Verde until some years later, as the local Indians were somewhat hostile.

Archeological Investigations

The story of archeological investigations at Mesa Verde National Park is not included in this publication. So much work has been accomplished since 1906, it would be impossible to adequately summarize it and to recognize all the scientists who have contributed so much effort, knowledge, and skill in gathering data that has helped reconstruct the life of the ancient Anasazi. While a number of works on Mesa Verde archeology have been published, a single publication on the total effort remains a future endeavor.

Bibliographical References

Ambler, J. Richard.
1977   *The Anasazi, Prehistoric People of the Four Corners Region.* Museum of Northern Arizona, Flagstaff, Arizona.

Breternitz, David A., Arthur H. Rohn and Elizabeth A. Morris.
1974   *Prehistoric Ceramics of the Mesa Verde Region.* Museum of Northern Arizona, Ceramic Series No. 5, Flagstaff, Arizona.

Erdman, James A., Charles L. Douglas and John W. Marr.
1969   *Environment of Mesa Verde National Park.* Archaeological Research Series Number 7-B, National Park Service, Washington.

Hayes, Alden C.
1964   *The Archaeological Survey of Wetherill Mesa.* Archaeological Research Series Number 7-A, National Park Service, Washington.

Hayes, Alden C., and James A. Lancaster.
1975   *Badger House Community: Mesa Verde National Park.* Archaeological Research Series Number 7-E, National Park Service, Washington.

Hoben, Patricia.
1966   *The Establishment of Mesa Verde as a National Park.* Master's Thesis, University of Oklahoma, Norman, Oklahoma.

Jackson, W. H.
1924   First Official Visit to the Cliff Dwellings. *The Colorado Magazine,* Vol. 1, No. 4, May 1924, pp. 151-159, Colorado Historical Society, Denver.

Lancaster, James A., Jean M. Pinkley, Phillip Van Cleave and Don Watson.
1950   *Archaeological Excavations in Mesa Verde National Park, Colorado, 1950.* Archaeological Research Series, Number 2, National Park Service, Washington.

Lister, Robert H.
1968   *Archaeology for the Layman and Scientists at Mesa Verde.* Science, American Association for Advancement of the Sciences, Vol. 160.

National Parkways. Breternitz, David A. and Jack E. Smith.
1972   *Mesa Verde and Rocky Mountain National Parks.* National Parks Division of World Wide Research and Publishing Company, Casper, Wyoming.

Newman, William, A.
1975   *Geologic Time.* U.S. Department of the Interior, Geological Survey, INF-70-1, Washington.

Nordenskiöld, G.
1893   *The Cliff Dwellers of the Mesa Verde, Southwestern Colorado.* P. A. Norstedt & Soner, Stockholm.

Reyes, Ricardo Torres.
1970   *Mesa Verde National Park, An Administrative History, 1906-1970.* Office of History and Historic Architecture, National Park Service, Washington.

Rohn, Arthur H.
1971   *Mug House, Mesa Verde National Park, Colorado.* Archaeological Research Series, Number 7-D, National Park Service, Washington.

Rohn, Arthur H.
1963   Prehistoric Soil and Water Conservation on Chapin Mesa, Southwestern Colorado. *American Antiquity,* Vol. 28, No. 4, pp. 441-455.

Rohn, Arthur H.
1977   *Cultural Continuity and Change on Chapin Mesa.* Regents Press of Kansas, Lawrence, Kansas.

Rudd, Clayton G., Editor.
1969   Mesa Verde National Park. *Naturalist,* Vol. 25, No. 2, Natural History Society of Minnesota, Minneapolis, Minnesota.

Swannack, Jervis D. Jr.
1969   *Big Juniper House, Mesa Verde National Park, Colorado.* Archaeological Research Series Number 7-C, National Park Service, Washington.

Trewartha, Glenn T.
1954   *An Introduction to Weather and Climate.* McGraw-Hill Book Company, New York.

Wanek, Alexander A.
1959   *Geology and Fuel Resources of the Mesa Verde Area Montezuma and La Plata Counties, Colorado.* Geological Survey, Bulletin 1072-M, Washington.

Wenger, Stephen R.
1976   *Flowers of Mesa Verde National Park.* Mesa Verde Museum Association, Inc., Mesa Verde National Park, Colorado.

Wormington, H. Marie.
1968   *Prehistoric Indians of the Southwest.* The Denver Museum of Natural History, Popular Series No. 7, Denver.

Glossary

A number of words relating to the various sciences used at Mesa Verde are defined for the benefit of readers who may not be familiar with their meaning as they pertain to this publication.

Anthropomorphic.
: Resembling or made to resemble a human form.

Artifact.
: Any object made by humans for a specific use.

Culture.
: The sum total of a way of living by a group of humans, transmitted from one group to another.

Contiguous.
: Joined in contact or touching (such as rooms built adjoining each other).

Ecosystem.
: A system formed by the interaction of a community of organisms with their environment.

Extended family.
: A special group consisting of the family nucleus and various near relatives.

Kinship.
: Family relationship.

Kiva.
: A large chamber, usually underground, in Pueblo villages; used for religious purposes.

Prehistoric.
: Pertaining to a period prior to recorded history.

Pueblo.
: Referring to (1) a style or type of home, usually multistoried, of stone or adobe, (2) a member of a group of Indians living in the Southwest, or (3) a town or village.

Sequence.
: The progression of one thing or period after another.

Site.
: The location of a house or village in its environment.

Special societies.
: A group of persons associated for certain religious, benevolent, or other purposes.

Credits

Page	Title	Source
8	Geological Time Scale	U.S. Geological Survey
12	Aerial view of canyons	National Park Service
21	Moccasin Mesa Fire	Stephen R. Wenger
34	Pithouse floor plan	National Park Service
41	Morefield kiva	University of Colorado
58	Step House plan	National Park Service
76	Fewkes	NPS Collection
77	Two Story Cliff House	W. H. Jackson/NPS Collection
78	Jackson Group	W. H. Jackson/NPS Collection
79	Wetherills	NPS Collection
79	Acowitz	NPS Collection
79	Cliff Palace	NPS Collection
80	Wetherills in Spruce Tree	NPS Collection
81	Relics	George Beam
82-83	Nordenskiöld photographs	Nordenskiöld 1891/NPS Collection
84	Nordenskiöld excavated artifacts	Gustaf Nordenskiöld
85	Virginia McClurg	Photographer unknown
86	Lucy Peabody	Photographer unknown
86-89	First transportation in the park	NPS Collection
87	Nusbaum	NPS Collection
88	CCC building museum	NPS Collection
90	Early Park accommodations	NPS Collection
92	Two Story Cliff House	W. H. Jackson/NPS Collection

GRAPHIC DESIGN: Nancy Leach – Graphic Interpretations, Durango, Colorado
ILLUSTRATIONS: David W. Wilson – The Art Department, Durango, Colorado
TYPOGRAPHER: Jack Klein – Jack Rabbit Type, Durango, Colorado
COLOR SEPARATIONS: L&M Printing, Denver, Colorado
LITHOGRAPHER: Imperial Litho & Dryography, Phoenix, Arizona